Frederick Stonehouse

Haunted Lakes II

More Great Lakes Ghost Stories

Lake Superior Port Cities Inc.

First Edition: September 2000

5 4 3 2

 LAKE SUPERIOR PORT CITIES INC.
P.O. Box 16417
Duluth, Minnesota 55816-0417
USA   888-BIG LAKE (244-5253)

Publishers of *Lake Superior Magazine* and
Lake Superior Travel Guide

Library of Congress Cataloging-In-Publication Data

Stonehouse, Frederick.
    Haunted lakes II : more Great Lakes ghost stories /
        Frederick Stonehouse. – 1st ed.
        p. cm.
    Includes bibliographical references (p.) and index.
    ISBN 0-942235-39-8
    1. Ghosts – Great Lakes Region. 2. Sea monsters – Great Lakes.
        I. Title: Haunted lakes
    2. II. Title: Haunted lakes two. III. Title.

    BF1472.U6 S765 2000
    133.1'0977 – dc21   00-061506

Printed in the United States of America

    Editing: Paul L. Hayden, Konnie LeMay, Hugh E. Bishop
    Design: Mathew Pawlak
Cover Art: Gary Lundstrom
    Printing: Sheridan Books Inc., Chelsea, Michigan

To my wonderful wife, Lois

Introduction

Whether you choose to believe any of these tales is essentially immaterial. What is important is their acceptance as maritime folklore of the Great Lakes. They are part of the social history of the Lakes.

Sailors of the past were much closer to the mysteries of nature. Events like the Northern Lights, St. Elmo's Fire and white squalls were less well understood and formed the basis for many superstitions and beliefs. Today, as a result of our reliance on "science," our daily folklore is all but gone. Since we "know" the "why" of these unusual phenomenon, we no longer accept the old invented reasons.

By contrast, ghosts seem more widely accepted than ever before. TV programs about the supernatural are commonplace, as are books and other publications. It seems the more we move into the new millennium of high science and technology, the more we seek answers in the old millennium of spirits and ghosts.

Ghost stories and tales of the "unusual" appear to be a resource without end. Everyone has a favorite yarn. Some were handed down through generations and others retold from popular books. Some are even the result of firsthand experience. It is this last group that is most fascinating. It seems everyone sailing the lakes, from commercial mariners to weekend boaters, all have their own anecdotes of the unexplained. My experience has been that every lighthouse has its own story, every island its own spirits and every desolate stretch of beach has lonely shades that haunt the shore.

The original *Haunted Lakes,* as published in 1997, has been very well received in the Great Lakes community. People enjoyed reading stories about the old superstitions, sea serpents and ghosts of the Great Lakes. It touched an area rarely explored.

Since its publication, many people have pointed me to new tales and related their personal experiences with forces from the beyond. There was clearly enough material for a *Haunted Lakes II.* As in *Haunted Lakes,* these stories are all "factual" or at least as factual as such things can be, given the inability to apply any sort of verifying criteria.

People ask whether I believe in ghosts. In reply, I dodge the question by saying that there are things that I don't understand. Whether they are called ghosts, spirits, shades or other paranormal monikers, something is there, something we do not fully understand. Perhaps someday we will comprehend what it is, but for now it is all a mystery.

When all is said and done, please remember that, although this material is not history, it is clearly part of the wonderfully rich and varied fabric of our Great Lakes maritime past. It is our heritage.

Frederick Stonehouse
September 2000

Contents

CHAPTER 1

Lighthouse Ghosts

The Ghosts of Seul Choix Point

The two women were working in the gift shop of the old lighthouse, putting books on the sales shelves, checking the cash box, doing the myriad of small things necessary to open for the tourists sure to visit during the day. Suddenly the woman nearest the door to the parlor looked up and sniffed the air.

"Do you smell something burning? Boy, is it ever strong!"

The other woman hurried out from behind the counter and into the parlor. "Yes, it's cigar smoke all right. It hasn't been this strong in a long time. I wonder if it means anything?"

The first woman replied, "Oh, it's just the captain visiting. He will not be here long."

This scene, or ones like it, have been enacted frequently at the Seul Choix Point Lighthouse, which has a reputation as one of the most haunted lights on the Great Lakes.

Seul Choix Point Lighthouse is located in Gulliver, Michigan, at the end of a small peninsula jutting into Lake Michigan known as Seul Choix Point (pronounced Sis Shwa). The light is about 60 miles west of the Straits of Mackinac. The name roughly translates to "only choice." It was the only harbor, however small, that the old French voyageurs found as a safe refuge along this long and open stretch of northern Lake Michigan shore.

Work on the lighthouse started in 1886, when Congress appropriated the money, but a series of delays, including rebuilding the tower, meant that the station did not open until September

Seul Choix Point Lighthouse. AUTHOR'S COLLECTION

1895. The 79-foot tower was originally fitted with a third order Fresnel lens that projected a beam 17 miles out into the inky blackness. Today an airport beacon has replaced it.

A two-story brick keeper's building is attached to the tower. A brick rear addition was added in 1925, which allowed the building to house both the families of keeper and his assistant. A foghorn building, two oil houses and an assistant keeper's residence complete the principal structures on the grounds.

From 1895 until 1973, it continued as a manned light station, first by the old Lighthouse Service and, after 1939, by the Coast Guard. Nothing much out of the ordinary happened at Seul Choix Point. There were no great storms or shipwrecks. Keepers and their families came and went, as did the inevitable lighthouse inspectors. All was quiet and peaceful.

After the Coast Guard left in 1973, no longer keeping men on site, the light was still maintained as an active beacon, but the buildings have deteriorated significantly. When the Gulliver Historical Society took over the structures in 1988, considerable repairs were needed. It was during this work that the society discovered that the lighthouse wasn't really empty. There were "others" living in the light!

Much of the initial restoration work was done by inmates from Camp Manistique Prison under contract to the society. On several

2

occasions inmates refused to go upstairs, claiming they "felt the presence of something supernatural up there."

Some months afterward, a team of carpenters was hired to install floor tile in the kitchen and hallway. The work went along without interruption until it was nearly done. To finish the job, one man came to the light alone on a bright and windless spring day. He let himself in, then carefully locked the door behind him. Although the light was still closed for the winter season, sometimes tourists would show up anyway. It was best to keep the doors locked in order to work uninterrupted.

He was kneeling on the floor in the parlor at the base of the stairs to the second floor. As he started to nail the subfloor he heard the clear sound of someone walking in the upstairs hallway. When he stopped hammering, the foot steps stopped. When he started, they began again. At first the workman assumed he was hearing a weird echo from his hammering. Just to be sure no one was upstairs, he yelled, "Who's there?" Since he received no answer, he again checked the locked doors assuring that he was alone, then went back to work, continuing to hammer the subfloor. The sound of footsteps returned, walking again across the upstairs floor. He stopped work to listen, expecting the steps to stop, too. They didn't! The heavy steps continued to march across the floor above, then

The dining room table with the mysterious moving silverware. AUTHOR'S COLLECTION

started to come slowly down the stairs. Frightened by the unknown, he quickly grabbed his tools and ran from the lighthouse. He refused to come back alone to finish the job!

One of the most common ghostly manifestations at Seul Choix Point Light is the pungent, almost nauseating stench of cigar smoke. It is most common in the parlor around the base of the stairs, but also has been detected in the upstairs hall. One time, two visitors ran downstairs and into the gift shop and told the tour guide they were sure the lighthouse was on fire. There was a terrible smoky stench upstairs. Perhaps the wiring was burning or someone had tossed a lit cigar into a bedroom. When the guide checked, everything was normal. The ghost had struck again.

Just opposite the parlor is a dining room which is a re-creation of the dining room in the lighthouse at the turn of the 20th century. Working from an old photograph, the society strived hard to make it as accurate as possible. An antique round oak table set with original china, stemware and silverware settings has become an active spot for ghostly action. The round table was the only piece of furniture that was authentic to the lighthouse. It was discovered scattered in the basement. Was there a reason why no one wanted it? Or, why was it left in pieces? The rest of the furniture was borrowed from nearby residences.

Silverware on the table has been known to "move." A curator will set it properly at night and the next morning it will be found reversed. When the silverware is discovered rearranged, it is often with the forks set upside down. This is an old English custom and Captain Joseph Townshend, whose ghost is suspected of being the principal haunt, was born in Bristol, England. Also a family Bible left open was found completely closed in the morning. Since the pages are heavy paper and there is no draft, some other force must be at work. Was Captain Townshend closing a chapter of his life by closing the Bible?

In June 1997, a TV crew from Saginaw, Michigan, visited the lighthouse to do a documentary on its restoration. They were not there to focus on the ghosts. While they were there, however, they did have a number of strange experiences.

The TV crew was given a tour of the lighthouse by Marilyn Fischer, the president of the Gulliver Historical Society, then taken out to the fog signal building where there were additional historical displays. Unknown to anyone else, the cameraman rearranged the stack of sheet music on the piano, switching the top music to "Blue Spanish Eyes." No one else knew of the change. When the group

The pages of the Bible turned as if by an unseen hand. AUTHOR'S COLLECTION

left the lighthouse, the doors were locked tight. Even though it was early evening, tourists still visited the park grounds and since the tour guides were gone for the day, it was necessary to lock the building. After touring the fog signal building, the group returned to the lighthouse. The cameraman immediately asked who had been in the building? Marilyn Fischer replied that no one had. The man was insistent that someone had been in the house. Fischer again replied that no one had been, that the guides were gone and she had the only keys. The man then explained about the changing sheet music. He had left "Blue Spanish Eyes" on top and now it was "For Whom the Bell Tolls." Obviously someone had come in and changed the music sheets. Fischer explained the illogic of it all. If the cameraman was the only person who knew about the music, then whether anyone came into the lighthouse or not was immaterial since only *he* knew about the music. The unanswered question was who shifted the music back? When the cameraman realized the implications of Fischer's statements, "his eyeballs got as big as saucers!" The sheet music changed position three times throughout the evening, as did the silverware on the round table.

Three members of the TV crew and a clairvoyant and his wife all slept that evening in their sleeping bags on the hard parlor floor. Five times during the night the crew smelled pungent cigar smoke. Each instance lasted for perhaps a minute. It was sickening enough that one of the members was pushed to her limit and ready to leave the building for a motel.

The crew also observed and videotaped mysterious hologram-like images in an upstairs bedroom mirror. The mirror would suddenly cloud up with a boiling vapor effect, resolve itself into two faces and finally fade away into nothing. One of the faces seemed to transform itself into a skull-like image before disappearing. The second face had bushy eyebrows, mustache and beard, with a long nose. Old-timers often claimed that if a mirror wasn't covered when there was a death in the house, the victim's spirit will move into the mirror. Is this what happened at Seul Choix Point?

The film crew left a video camera "on," aimed at the stairway all night in the hope of recording any supernatural activity. Inexplicably the video portion failed, although the audio recorded a bizarre "whooshing" sound. There was no logical explanation for either the camera that had worked fine all day malfunctioning or for the strange sound.

The next morning, one of the cameramen was setting up his gear in the upstairs bedroom when he flippantly remarked, "OK, Mr. Ghost, let's stop playing games. Make your presence known." A harsh odor immediately overcame him, making him physically ill for the rest of the morning.

The bedroom with the ghostly mirror. AUTHOR'S COLLECTION

Another videographer was shooting video at the lighthouse for a historic documentary when he, too, experienced a spooky incident. He was outside at night looking inside through a window when he saw a dark shadowy figure walk across the hall near the parlor. A quick search revealed that no one was inside the locked lighthouse. Had he actually seen the ghost?

Marilyn Fischer has done extensive work in trying to determine just who the ghost may be. Her best estimate is that it is Captain Joseph Willy Townshend, the lightkeeper from 1902 to 1910. Born in England, he spent the first 16 years of his working life sailing salt water. After immigrating to the United States, he initially entered a Presbyterian seminary but dropped out in less than a year. He worked on the Mackinac Island docks for a while, then as an engineer on a lightship. In 1901, he became keeper at Seul Choix Point. He seems to have the best connection to the supernatural activities.

Captain Townshend died at the light at age 65 on August 10, 1910, and was buried in the Manistique cemetery. The local newspaper reported that "many visitors and friends came by boat to attend the funeral and his children came all the way from Marquette." It was said he died a very painful death in an upstairs bedroom. The body was quickly embalmed in the basement of the lighthouse and prepared for burial. Placed in a rough cedar casket, he was laid out in the downstairs parlor for viewing. The traditional copper pennies were placed on the eyes to keep them shut. Because of the distance his family had to travel, the body was kept in the parlor for a longer period than normal. A granddaughter, now in her 90s, remembers attending her grandfather's funeral while just a child. Her only memories were watching a flickering oil lamp on top of a "lace covered table and viewing the coffin with a white haired man inside. He had bushy eyebrows, mustache and beard."

It is thought the bedroom he died in is the one with the strange, boiling mirror. Is there a connection? Was the mirror not covered and somehow his spirit was caught in it's vortex?

Lighthouses can be romantic places and Seul Choix is no different. In 1995, the lighthouse hosted the first wedding since 1936 when a keeper's son was married inside it 65 years earlier. For the 1995 wedding, one of the family members visited the light to consider how best to place the myriad of flowers needed for decoration. While sitting in the parlor on a warm and still evening, the woman was struck by a sudden blast of cold air, followed by a sickening aroma of pungent cigar smoke. Undaunted by the

Captain Joseph Willy Townshend and family. GULLIVER HISTORICAL SOCIETY

experience, the woman looked through the house but found no one. Returning to the parlor, she again sat down and once again was hit by the cold air and nauseating smoke. Enough was enough. She quickly left, the flowers be damned!

Not long ago, a woman new to the area drove to the lighthouse just to see what was there and had a ghostly encounter. "I was in the car with my husband, taking a ride for the day, and we decided to visit the Seul Choix Point Lighthouse. My husband was driving and I was enjoying the scenery along Lake Michigan. As we approached the parking lot at the entrance to the lighthouse park, I looked over at a small clearing in the woods and noticed an old man leaning against a tree. He had a bushy white beard and eyebrows and was dressed in a dark blue uniform with matching hat. He was just standing there staring out into nowhere. I blinked my eyes because it was such a strange sight and he was gone. He disappeared, just that fast! I looked around as we parked, but he was nowhere in sight!

"As we got out of the car, I told my husband about what I had just seen and we shrugged it off, thinking maybe it was someone in costume, doing a re-enactment. We had a great tour of the lighthouse and inside on a mannequin, I saw what a real lightkeeper's uniform looked like. Before we left I knew for sure that the uniform the old man had on was a lightkeeper's!

"It was always in the back of my mind … what became of the old man? Then several months later my father saved a newspaper for me to read. As I picked the paper up, there was a picture of the old man whom I had seen outside the lighthouse. When I read the story, I immediately got cold chills all over my body and I couldn't believe my eyes! It was a story about the ghost of Seul Choix Point! The man I had seen leaning against the tree and the man in the picture were the exact same! *I knew for sure that I had seen the lighthouse ghost.*"[1]

Another visitor was standing in the upstairs hallway in the middle of a hot summer day when she was hit by a blast of cold air. She thought it strange to find such cold air in the building and remarked about it to a tour guide. "Why did they have air conditioning only in the upstairs hallway? Was it to preserve antiques?" Considering that the lighthouse has no air conditioning, was it the captain on the prowl?

Another visitor walking around the grounds of the lighthouse reported briefly seeing a man with a white beard and dark suit looking out the upstairs window of the "mirror" bedroom. Who was it?

The ghosts evidently predate the Gulliver Historical Society's acquisition of the property. One of the men who acted as a caretaker and lived in the lighthouse, between the time of Coast Guard abandonment and society procurement, reported that he and his family sometimes saw unidentified figures in the upstairs windows.

Unexplained things happened in the house, too. Another man who was one of the last Coast Guard lightkeepers claimed there were ghosts in the house while he was there. He remembered particular problems cleaning the old Fresnel lens. He would carefully clean until it was spotless only to return later and find fingerprints on it. He was alone at the time! Who, or what, was leaving the fingerprints?

The lighthouse was visited by a clairvoyant before its recent ghostly reputation became known. The first time the man entered the house and walked upstairs, he quickly ran back out saying, "I have to get out of here!" He started to hyperventilate and it took a while to regain his composure. Apparently he was driven out by the result of the strong psychic energy within the house. Several years later when he very cautiously went back in, he determined that,

9

"Someone had died a terrible death," but what he felt was, "not a bad spirit." This has been taken as a reference to Captain Townshend's death. When the clairvoyant walked into the back display room, he detected a strong presence under the ceiling trapdoor in the hallway, implying there was another entity in the attic. No one ever went up to see!

In June 1997, Jack Edwards of *Great Lakes Cruiser* Magazine led a team to the lighthouse to investigate the reported haunting. Making the connection between smelling cigar smoke and cigars, Jack positioned cigars in strategic places in the house. One was placed in an upstairs bedroom and another in the "mirror" bedroom. A third went on the corner post on the lower staircase and the last on the dining room table. The team then rolled out their sleeping bags on the parlor floor and sacked out for the night. The next morning the corner post cigar and dining room cigar were missing. Those upstairs were unmoved. The forks on the dining room table had also been repositioned. Where the cigars had gone was a mystery until several hours later when they were discovered in the breast pocket of lighthouse keeper Ronald Rosie's uniform. The uniform was displayed on a mannequin in the dining room next to the round oak table. As if to mark their location, the uniform cap was now backwards!

The latest incident at Seul Choix Point occurred on April 16, 1999. Eagle scouts Joel Norton and Mike Ozanich were both doing term papers on the subject of ghosts and they requested permission to spend a night in the lighthouse. Scoutmaster Jim Barr agreed to stay with them as a supervisor. All spread out their sleeping bags on the parlor floor. Following the lead of the cigars, they offered the ghost three different priced stogies, the most expensive costing $8. Each was placed in a different location.

When their adventure was finished, each cigar had moved, with the exception of the $8 one. Perhaps it was just too good for the ghost's jaded taste! One cigar moved room to room, from the dining room table to the kitchen table. A cigar on the upper staircase newel post moved to the lower newel post. Both a knife and spoon on the dining room table changed position. Three or four times during the night, the scouts detected a rotting smell in different isolated areas of the house. It quickly dissipated. Joel's video camera refused to work, even with new batteries. Later, it worked fine.

At one point, Scoutmaster Barr watched a dark bird-like shadow fly across the full length of the dining room. He later said,

"The spirit at the lighthouse is doing funny tricks or pranks! It's like he didn't want anybody else in the house! The boys were scared half to death – they never left my side!" By 5 a.m. Saturday, the scouts left the lighthouse, having their fill of the ghost's strange tricks.

The whole area around Seul Choix Point is rife with wandering spirits. Just down the road from the lighthouse and past the old Indian graveyard are several houses reported to be haunted. The area was first settled by French-Canadians and many took up the commercial fishing trade. Perhaps it is the old fishermen who still haunt the area.

The first two houses are side-by-side and less than 100 yards from an old commercial fishing harbor. One house is home to the ghost of an Indian woman who apparently had bad experiences in the house. Treated harshly, her spirit simply remained after death.

In one instance a father and son were sitting around the kitchen table when the father noticed that the clock on the wall was broken. Tired of the old clock's problems, he told his son to get rid of it, to take it into the swamp and throw it as far as he could. Later that day the son did exactly as he was told and was rewarded with a loud splash. Two days later the father, son and a neighbor were sitting around the same table when the father noticed that the clock was still hanging on the wall. Irritated, the father asked his son why he didn't get rid of it as he was told? The son swore that he had thrown it into the swamp two days earlier! Rattled by the returning clock, the neighbor left immediately, never to set foot in the house again.

Is the ghostly Captain Townshend still "keeping the light?" AUTHOR'S COLLECTION

The two houses where spirits are said to roam. AUTHOR'S COLLECTION

In another instance a young boy was returning from hunting when he experienced a ghostly encounter. "I came home from school one day. I used to come down and go hunting different places and I came here this day, had Spot with me, a little cocker. I was here hunting rabbits. My uncle had lived over here, but had moved away. There was nobody here. I shot two or three rabbits and was starting home and I got right here. I looked up in the window and there was a woman standing up there, a real pretty woman. I couldn't figure out why. There wasn't anybody there. Everyone was supposed to be gone. I got a cold feeling. I went home and never said nothing to anyone. I kinda forgot a little bit. I brought it up to my mother and asked her about it. She said, 'You never know. Things have been seen and heard down there. You don't know who it was, if it was anybody.'

"They had people down there, a priest to bless the homes. Then they had someone back with another priest. They said it was rock spirits. I never said anything to anyone until maybe a year ago. My dad's aunt who lived next door, Aunt Liza, had a niece, Benice's daughter. Her name was Agnes May. But she didn't live in that house. She lived in the other house. She died of TB. I always thought it might have been her. She was a pretty girl. That girl was a pretty girl. That girl was pretty just like her. But I don't know why she would be in that house. When she lived in that house, I don't know. She was the most beautiful thing I ever seen. I haven't seen others like her yet!"

Who was the mysterious woman in the window?

Two men and their children were sitting at the kitchen table on a hot and still summer day when the iron regulator in the unlit wood stove began to spin. Slowly at first, it increased speed until they could not follow the motion. Suddenly, the middle cast-iron lid leaped into the air, turning over several times and nearly reaching the ceiling before returning to the exact position from which it started. The regulator slowed movement and stopped.

A young bride and her husband were living in the house when another spooky incident occurred. Shortly after moving into the house, the bride was in the kitchen when she heard a lot of movement and footsteps upstairs. Thinking her house guests had finally awakened, she prepared a beautiful breakfast then leaned up the stairway and yelled, "Come and get it." No one came down.

When she finally went upstairs to see what was keeping her guests, she found the rooms empty! Sometime later her husband and guests came home from a long walk on the beach. So who was upstairs? She didn't want to know! The husband and his wife moved out soon afterward.

While exterior repairs were recently being done to the house, strange noises like glass breaking and footsteps and dreadful odors came from inside. When checked, nothing was ever amiss. What was going on inside the old house?

It is said that during the renovations of this century-old house, a secret attic was discovered. Sealed within were old tins, trunks, fishing equipment, calendars from 1930-36, clothes and school books. It was like a time capsule. Why had the room been sealed shut? Was it an effort to keep something inside and undisturbed?

Tearing up the old kitchen floor revealed a trap door leading to several mysterious underground chambers. The walls of the rooms were tongue-and-groove plank and the floors sand. Part was evidently an old cold cellar used in the days before refrigeration to keep food fresh. Cans of preserved fish and berries were found dating from the 1920s. In one of the small chambers, what were believed to be human bones from a young girl were discovered buried in the sand. The room was immediately resealed. The owners wanted to leave well enough alone!

The same clairvoyant who visited the lighthouse also examined the haunted houses. He confirmed the presence of numerous spirits and said one of the rooms in the north house was being used as a "guest room," that many spirits passed through it, staying only briefly. He explained that he felt nothing but happy spirits within.

On this same visit, the clairvoyant started to walk the grounds surrounding the old houses. All of a sudden, he explained a shooting that had taken place on the shores of Lake Michigan in a grouping of tar-paper shacks. He saw the spot where a dead body was found. What he was seeing was the famous "murder at Seul Choix Point" – the Pond versus Blanchard shooting that took place on June 18, 1859. Ironically the date that the clairvoyant visited the area was exactly June 18, almost a century and a half later. Did a porthole in time briefly open to view this page from the past?

While building the foundation for a nearby pole barn, a worker dug up a small handcarved brass cross and two tin coffin plates. One was engraved with "Our Darling" and the other "Our Loved One." Scraping the ground a little deeper he found part of a girl's leather shoe, obviously handmade by a cobbler. He then stopped digging. Was there an old grave along the shore? Whose was it? Is it connected to the mysterious goings on?

The house next door is haunted by unknown spirits, too. Once a man was sleeping in an upstairs bedroom when he was startled by a voice shouting, "Son of a bitch!" The man bolted upright and strained to hear more. Soft, subdued voices drifted up from downstairs, but were in a language he couldn't understand. Heavy footsteps echoed across the downstairs floor, too. Cabinet doors opened and slammed shut. The pet cat that was lying sleepily by his side suddenly arched his back and hissed. Silently the man crept downstairs to see what was going on. All he found was an empty house.

The two houses sit side-by-side on an old gravel road leading to the harbor. Once several people were eating at the kitchen table when they were startled to see a young woman in a long white flowing dress walking casually along the road from the beach and on past the houses. What astonished them was that they all recognized her from old photographs, and she had been dead for half a century! When they ran outside the girl had vanished into thin air.

The third house is much newer, but equally plagued by ghosts. The reason for the haunting could be its location, right on the old wagon trail along the lakeshore. A previous owner said he could sit in his easy chair watching TV and at the same time look down a hallway toward the bedrooms. Every so often he would see various sized black figures moving across the hallway, actually passing

Do ghostly forms still travel the old coach road? AUTHOR'S COLLECTION

"through" his walls and house. They never made a sound and seemed to travel in groups. He also never said anything about these "travelers" to his wife. However, one day she sat in "his" chair and saw the baffling figures. After he confirmed seeing them too, she insisted on moving out of the house. She wasn't going to share her home with anyone else!

Supposedly the couple was seeing "rock spirits," ghostly black shapes that would float mysteriously over the rocks along the Lake Michigan shore. For two centuries, local fishermen have claimed to see them while coming ashore from a long day with their nets. Priests were called in who said they were not evil, but the men of the cloth still hung crosses and rosaries in the trees wherever the shapes were seen. It is thought that these rock spirits are simply continuing their ancient trek along the old trail. In this case, they are just passing directly through a structure that wasn't there 200 years ago. Do they represent a group of early travelers, perhaps a family, who met death on the trail and today are simply trying to finish their interrupted journey? Or are they something else, perhaps the spirits of an ancient people still making their way along the lonely shore?

I visited the lighthouse in October 1997 and was given an excellent tour and interview by Marilyn Fischer. While there, nothing supernatural happened. The cigars I had planted in

15

different places failed to disappear, the silverware stayed in place and there was no pungent aroma of burning stogies. In short, everything was as it should be – or at least I thought so at the time.

It is my habit when interviewing people to use a micro recorder to capture their comments on tape. People talk faster than I can take notes and this assures me of a higher degree of accuracy. I recorded much of my interview with Marilyn Fischer on my micro recorder. Later, when I got home I took the tape out of the machine, labeled it and filed it with all the material concerning Seul Choix Point Light. When I got down to writing the piece, I would play the tape. In February 1998, I was ready to write. I did the initial draft based on my notes and other research material, then played the tape to flesh out the details. The tape was good quality, with Marilyn's comments clear and understandable. There was also something more on the tape, an eerie, low moaning sound that made the hair on the back of my neck stand up! There was no such sound when I recorded the interview, but it's there now! I have no idea what caused it. It never happened before. However, considering the highly charged psychic atmosphere where I was using it, it fits right in doesn't it?[2]

The Lighthouse

This story was given to me by a sailor of long experience. To my knowledge, neither he nor his wife have any psychic powers. Both refuse to name the island and are steadfast that its real location remains a secret. I did draw out of them, however, that it is in Lake Superior. More than that they would not reveal, only calling it "Rock Island." I think they really want others to have the same thrills they did in discovering such a real Great Lakes mystery.

It was great sailing on the lake, a good breeze from the northeast and we were making a fast nine knots. I even had the big jenny up! It was only my wife and me on this trip. We looked forward to this late season trip for a long time, a week on the big lake with no phones or kids. Grandma took care of the last part and the office would just have to suffer without us.

We never stayed at Rock Island, but when we studied the charts over the winter planning this trip, it looked like a wonderfully out-of-the-way place to tuck in for a day or so. It had a good deep water channel leading into a little cove right behind the island. Once inside, it looked to be proof against all winds.

As we approached it in late afternoon, the old lighthouse stood out plainly against the rock of the island. Our pilot book said it was no longer in use and I remember reading somewhere that it was abandoned back before World War II when the shipping lanes changed. Today it didn't even have one of those silly little plastic lens on the tower.

We dropped the sails, fired up the kicker and started for the island. When we got closer, my wife slipped up to the pulpit and, using hand signals, helped me work through the channel and into the little cove behind the island. She released the hook and we found it had

The Lighthouse had a life of its own. ART BY CARL GAWBOY, LAKE SUPERIOR MAGAZINE

pretty good bottom, probably sand from the feel of it. I decided a single moor would do with the calm forecast and as sheltered as we were from the winds. Sitting in the cockpit, we could just see the upper part of the lighthouse over the trees.

The island looked so damn intriguing that we grabbed a couple of beers from the reefer and went ashore in the rubber dingy. The crib dock was still partially intact, probably because of its sheltered location, so we were able to get ashore dry. The nearby boathouse had not fared as well. Snow had collapsed the roof and it was mostly just a pile of rubble. I found a small path up through the woods toward the lighthouse and, after 20 minutes or so, we came out on the edge of a little clearing. The lighthouse stood on the northern edge of it, right where the rocks shelved down toward the water. From this angle the lighthouse was especially impressive. The brick building was a story and a half with a tower 70-feet or so in height attached to the west side. Once the whole structure was covered in whitewash, but today the red brick was completely exposed. All the windows were boarded up. A small brick oil house was off to the east. We walked over to the lighthouse and I tried the door but it refused to open. Half a dozen nails protruded from the frame showing the reason.

The sun was starting to set, so we returned to the boat. I had heard there was an old graveyard on the east end of the island. Tomorrow I would go look for it. Supposedly, it held the bodies of half a dozen sailors lost in a turn of the century shipwreck. The island, lighthouse and graveyard would make a nice story. I do a little writing and hate to pass up a good tale.

We had a late dinner and afterwards enjoyed a magnificent display of the northern lights. Sitting in the cockpit with a glass of wine and my arm around my wife, life just couldn't get much better. There weren't even any bugs! I glanced from the stars to the northern lights to the beacon rotating slowly, its beam cutting through the night.

What the hell! That isn't right. The lighthouse is abandoned. What is going on? I asked my wife if she saw what I did. She said yes, the light was on! Could it be a strange reflection of the sun, based maybe on the height of the tower and the angle of the sun past the apparent horizon? However wild that theory, it would not explain the crisp rotation. From what we could see the light was in full operation.

For at least two hours we alternated between watching the northern lights and the old lighthouse. Around midnight, it blinked off. Tired of coming up with useless theories, we rolled into our bunks. We couldn't solve the mystery that night anyway.

The next day we went back to the island and on up to the lighthouse. The building was sealed solid, every window and both front and back doors too! No one had gotten into it. The lamp room windows were also covered with black plywood sheets. Even if light were inside, it wasn't getting outside.

Feeling that there was nothing more to see at the lighthouse, we went looking for the graveyard. After a couple of hours crashing around in the underbrush, we found a small clearing bordered with the remnant of a wooden picket fence. There were no headstones, only half a dozen shallow depressions in the ground. Either the wooden coffins had collapsed or the bodies had been disinterred and returned to families. It was another mystery.

We spent the afternoon fishing and got a couple of nice lake trout. After an exhilarating swim in the cool water of the cove, I fired up the rail grill and my wife uncorked a bottle of Chablis.

Nothing tasted better than grilled trout and a fine dry Chablis. The northern lights didn't show that night, but the lighthouse beam did. Shortly after dark, it again cut through the starry sky.

I resolved to try to solve the mystery. We took the dingy to the island and, flashlights in hand, made our way up the trail. At night everything looks different, even a little spooky. When we reached the clearing we saw something neither of us will ever forget.

Light streamed out of every window in the lighthouse! A steady beam came out of the lamp room too! It was like the clock was turned back a century. We could see figures inside the house. There was one man with a full beard who walked past the kitchen window several times. There was also a woman and at least two children. We were perhaps 50 yards away, so we had a pretty fair view. The aroma of wood smoke hung heavy in the night air. The kitchen stove must have been fired up. At one point the woman came out the back door and yelled something. Pretty soon a big black dog came bounding out of the darkness and past her into the house. Illuminated by the light coming out the open door, we could see that the woman's hair was in a tight bun and she wore a long dress reaching down to her ankles. All of the figures looked absolutely solid, nothing vaporous or misty.

Despite what we were watching, there was no sense of fear. More than anything, it was a sense of curiosity. We watched for maybe an hour when I got too bold. I told my wife to stay in the trees and I crept up to the lighthouse to get a closer look. As I slowly worked my way through the clearing and up to the building, the furnishings inside came into better view. There was a big wood stove in the kitchen, pictures on the walls and lace on the windows. I almost reached the kitchen window when a small boy looked out and saw me. He pointed right at me, then said something. The bearded man appeared next to him, then everything went black. Bang, every light went off. By now I was close enough that my flashlight beam could reach the house and it showed that all the windows were boarded up tight, just as they had been during the day! When I turned around, my wife was right behind me. She said she didn't want me to have all the fun. I think she didn't want to wait in the bushes alone. We went back to the boat and, considering all we had seen, slept like babies.

The next morning we went back to the lighthouse, determined to give it a better examination. Everything was boarded up, heavy wood over the windows and doors nailed shut. I keep a large tool kit on the boat, complete with a small pry bar, which I now used to pull the nails out of the door. It creaked loudly as I slowly pushed it open. Inside was chaos, a combination of deterioration from the ravages of time and the work of an earlier generation of vandals, apparently done before the building was sealed up.

Our flashlights provided the only light, other than what came in through the open door and slits in the window boards. Inside, it was cold, almost freezing, in sharp contrast with the warmth outside. Peeling yellowed wallpaper hung down in great strips. In some places the plaster had fallen from the walls and ceiling, leaving lath visible like the bones of a prehistoric monster. Paper and other garbage littered the floor. Shattered glass from wine and whiskey bottles crunched underfoot.

In the dining room, chairs were overturned and the remnants of a table lay collapsed in the middle of the floor. Upstairs, two of the rooms still had beds and chests of drawers. The remains of a smashed child's china doll was in the corner of the smaller room. All the floors were coated in a thick layer of undisturbed gray dust.

It was evident that no one had been in here for a long time. Nothing we had found could in any stretch of the imagination explain what we had seen the previous night.

Our last stop was the kitchen. As we stood in the room talking, I leaned back, placing a hand on top of the wood stove. It was hot! Not hot enough to burn me, but hot enough to be uncomfortable. Touching it gingerly, my wife felt the same heat. When I opened the scuttle door, the coals were stone cold, as expected, after half a century since last being used. We fled the building!

I quickly nailed the door shut as best I could with my pry bar and we retreated to the boat. We hauled anchor and carefully threaded our way out the narrow channel and into the open lake to continue our trip. Looking back, we could see the old lighthouse looking down on us. I swear I saw someone standing on the gallery deck, but my wife said she saw nothing.

Neither of us can explain in the slightest what we saw and we both decided not to say where exactly it occurred. We just call it Rock Island. Regardless of what we experienced, it's still a beautiful spot. Our days there were wonderful ones and we feel another family is still enjoying their time there. There is no reason for anyone to ever disturb them.

A few years later we were at one of those cruising rendezvous and got to talking with the couple in the boat moored alongside. After drinks, the man asked if we had ever cruised around Rock Island. I admitted we had. Then he asked if we had ever moored in the little cove behind the island. I confirmed we had done that too. Finally, looking a little sheepish, he asked if we had seen anything "strange" while we were there? I looked at my wife and said, "No, nothing at all."

The Figure on the Beach

"The old guy I replaced was at the light for a long time, 30 years or so. Among the men in the old Coast Guard, he was a real legend, kind of an old man of the sea kind of thing. Anyway, when I arrived at the lighthouse he was still there. Normally, the keeper, especially one retiring, would be long gone, happy to finally be away from the damn place. But he was still there. He gave me the grand tour, showing me every little nook and cranny the old place had. It pretty much took the whole day.

"In late afternoon, we finally sat down for a cup of coffee. 'Bud,' he says, for some reason he called everybody 'Bud.'

"'Bud,' he says, 'I've seen many strange and wondrous things. You stay here long enough and you will, too. But you listen to me now, real close, 'cause this is important. Sometimes at night you will see something down on the beach. Just ignore it. Whatever you do, don't go near it, just stay away and it will stay away from you. If you bother it, you will regret it. I've lived with it for these 30 years and you can too, nice and easy, but should you do anything to it, I can't be responsible.'

"With that, he put down his coffee cup, picked up his old cane and hobbled out the door. My questions concerning what the hell he was talking about went unanswered.

"Everything went along fine for several months, then one dark November night, I was in the tower enjoying a good pipe and looked out toward the beach. I saw a dark shadow shifting over the sand. It moved down the beach slowly, as if searching for something in the wave wash. When it crossed the pale of the moon I could see it a little better. The form appeared human, but instead of walking normally, it moved somewhat hesitatingly, as if dragging a leg. I watched for a while, then it just disappeared. It was there, then it was gone!

"I didn't see it again until the spring of the following year. It followed the same routine as before, moving along the beach as if searching for something and lasting for 10 to 15 minutes before just fading away. One day, I asked the assistant keeper if he had ever seen anything out of the ordinary during the night watch. He said he didn't, everything was always the same.

21

"I saw it again in midsummer. It was the same as before, just walking along, then vanishing. I am not a brave man, but I had to find out what was going on. I resolved that the next time I would go down to the beach and have a closer look.

"In late fall, just before we would close for the season, it came again. I was ready for it and charged off to the beach with a flashlight. There was a break in the dunes directly in front of the lighthouse and that's where I reached the beach. I was only about 50 feet away when it loomed up in front of me. It was tall and dressed in rough clothes. The head was bare with a scraggly growth of black hair hanging down. The figure was still looking down to the sand and had not seen me.

"I switched on the flashlight and put the beam right on it and with a loud voice said, "Who are you? What are you looking for?" The figure stopped dead in its tracks and gazed up at me. The eyes glowed bright red. I'll never forget the eyes, the dreadful, burning eyes.

"The damn thing ran right for me! I took a couple of steps back and it kept coming. Then I turned and ran, not looking back until I got to the cut of the dunes. It was still coming right behind me! I ran straight into the lighthouse and slammed and bolted the door. For some reason I thought I was safe. The door started to shake, lightly at first then harder and more violently. The heavy door began to come apart in front of my eyes, to burst slowly if you can understand what I mean.

"I ran through the dining room and past my office to the door to the tower. I heard a loud crash and surmised it was the kitchen door shattering. All I could think of was to run up the tower with the hope that I could figure how to lock one of the scuttle doors behind me. I ran up the stairs as fast as I could, the creature pounding along behind me. I shot through the first scuttle and slammed it tight, then stood on it. When it reached it, the door just raised up into the air with me on top. I weigh almost 200 pounds, but it was as if I wasn't even there. I jumped off and ran up the last few steps to the lamproom and out to the gallery. As I burst out on the walkway, I could feel its breath. I ran to the left, hoping to get around the gallery and back inside and down the stairs before it got me. The door at the base of the tower was steel and could be bolted from the outside. Maybe it could contain it.

"Then a miracle happened. The first light of dawn broke over the horizon. Being that high up, with the ground still in darkness, the new light was in sharp contrast with the shadows of the night. The light evidently chased the figure off. I was suddenly conscious of being alone. It was gone!

"I never bothered the mysterious figure again and it never bothered me. I have no idea what it is, or what it is searching for, but I decided to take the old keeper's advice and just leave it alone."

The Lighthouse of Doom

The annals of lighthouse keeping are replete with stories of strange "doings," shadowy ghosts climbing steep and winding tower stairs, mysterious lights glimmering from the lamproom, phantom ships appearing off shore and unearthly sounds echoing through empty rooms. Certainly among the strangest tales is that of the St. Ignace Island Lighthouse on Lake Superior's rugged Canadian shore. Although its career was short, a mere six years, events at the little lighthouse were eerie enough that it quickly gained the reputation as the "lighthouse of doom."

Rational people can explain away the events that happened there as just an unfortunate chain of circumstances – bad luck and nothing more. But those who open their minds to a wider stream of consciousness, who accept that there are things that we don't always understand, perhaps will consider the idea that the damned place was truly cursed. Considering the fate of the only three lightkeepers ever appointed to St. Ignace Light, something was certainly wrong!

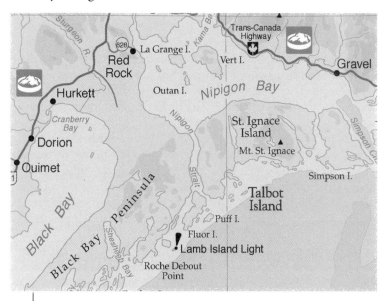

St. Ignace Lighthouse was built on Talbot Island.

St. Ignace Light was the first Canadian light built on Lake Superior. It was included in a group of six contracted for on June 6, 1866. Five were Lake Huron lights: two at Killarney on Georgian Bay, two at Little Current on Manitoulin Island and one at Clapperton Island. The last of the six was at St. Ignace Island, Lake Superior. It was intended that the six lights would provide a pathway from the major port of Collingwood, on Georgian Bay, through to the head of Lake Superior. Construction went quickly and all were finished in the summer of 1867. The American side of the lake was already comparatively well lit, with eight in operation by then. By contrast, settlement on the Canadian north shore was slow and demand for lights weak.

St. Ignace Light was actually built on Talbot Island, a small islet two miles to the south of the much larger St. Ignace Island. The long narrow island has a dense cover of scrub brush and heavy undergrowth despite the rocky soil. It is an extremely inhospitable location. The lighthouse was erected on the sloping southeast corner of the island, about 200 yards from the south shore and 500 yards from the east end. The foundation was rock and mortar, with three sides sloping into the angled rock which formed the fourth side of solid rock. As typical for a Canadian lighthouse of the period, the building was wood with a white square tower attached. The fixed white beam was provided by three mineral oil lamps. There were many dangerous reefs and shoals in the area and as trade expanded, the government thought the new light would be needed to guide ships safely past these hazards.

Canadian lighthouse authorities had a reputation of letting their keepers largely fend for themselves, especially regarding arrangements for leaving their stations in the fall. Considering that it was more than 200 miles to Sault Ste. Marie, the nearest major Canadian city, there was some perverse logic in this benign neglect. It was too far for a government boat to come just to remove a single keeper. They also wanted the keeper to maintain the light as long as possible, certainly at least to the close of navigation, so taking him off early was not an option. The result was that once the season ended, the man was left to his own devices to close the light and make his way to winter quarters.

The keeper for the first season was a Mr. Perry. Apparently he was a good and reliable man who did the job well. When the season ended in November, he carefully did all the many tasks necessary to secure the light for the long winter then left in an open boat for a Hudson's Bay Company post at Nipigon, more than 25 long miles to the north. He didn't make it. When spring came, his frozen body was discovered near his boat on the shores of Nipigon Bay. Exactly how he died is unknown. But the local men thought that he just froze to death trying to make the trip.

Undeterred, lighthouse authorities appointed Thomas Lamphier as the new keeper for the next season and he decided to bring his wife to the lonely little island. Lightkeeping was hard work, so he would welcome her help as well as company. To avoid Perry's mistake, he and his wife would winter on the island, instead of braving the fall storms in a mad dash to civilization.

Lamphier had sailed a Hudson's Bay Company schooner out of Fort William for 20 years, so he was familiar with the area and its many dangers. His wife was a native and also used to the "rough" conditions. They were the perfect couple to operate the light and to winter over on the island.

Then disaster struck. Lamphier became sick. Out on the desolate island, he was far beyond any kind of medical care. Despite his wife's best efforts, his condition deteriorated, he slowly weakened and finally died. Unlike in the terrible saga of Angeline and Charlie Mott on Isle Royale, there was no lack of food. Mrs. Lamphier would not be tempted to "consume" her husband as Angeline had been. The biggest problem was the lack of a burial ground on the rocky island. After carefully wrapping his body in a stiff canvas sail from the station boat, she laboriously dragged her husband out back and pushed him in a large crevice deep in the rocks. For the rest of the long dark winter she stood a lonely and forsaken vigil on the melancholy island.

Finally spring arrived and a group of Ojibway people stopped at the island and found the very distraught Mrs. Lamphier. They were shocked to learn of the keeper's death, but also to see the horrible condition of his wife. She was drawn and haggard, old before her time. Most striking was her hair. Jet black when she arrived at the island, it was now snow white! Considering the overwhelming need to bury the keeper, they removed the body from its temporary mausoleum and carried it to Bowman Island, about a mile to the north. At Bowman Island there was enough soil to dig a grave. Today the grave is marked by a simple white cross.

The records are somewhat sketchy, but apparently the next keeper was Andrew Hynes. The Canadian lighthouse authorities had learned nothing from the death of Perry. They still left it up to the individual keeper to make his way off the island to winter quarters. After closing the station in the fall of 1872, Hynes left the lighthouse by boat and headed for Silver Islet, 50 miles to the south. The entire route was over open lake. He must have fought storms and severe cold the whole distance, because 18 long days later he finally arrived at his destination, frostbitten and nearly starved. His reprieve was only temporary. Within days of his arrival he was dead. Old-timers blamed it on the tremendous hardships he endured. Others weren't so sure. After all, wasn't he the keeper at the lighthouse of doom?

After Hynes' death, the Canadians gave up on the lighthouse that had gained the terrible reputation. They knew the deadly fate of every keeper who went to man the light. Since sailing routes had already changed, the light was not as important as originally thought. The government abandoned it, stating that the lighthouse building would likely be moved to a better location. Perhaps thinking of its grisly reputation for killing keepers, they were happy just to leave it alone and forgotten.

The lighthouse may have been left unmanned by the government, but local fishermen continued to use it as a daymark. On foggy days when boats were still out on the lake, one of the men would pound on the wooden sides of the house with a log. The low booming sound was powerful enough to guide the missing boats back to safe harbor.

The same fishermen also believed that the old lighthouse was haunted. They claimed that on moonlit nights they could see the figure of a woman with long flowing white hair gliding through the trees as if searching for something. Although her soft calls were plainly heard over the quiet lake, they were never quite loud enough to be understood.

Today virtually nothing is left of the cursed lighthouse. There is still evidence of the rock-and-mortar foundation but little else. Wooden lighthouses were never built to endure. Powerful north storms simply tore it apart!

What, if anything, cursed the St. Ignace Light is open to conjecture, of course. Perhaps, as old-timers reasoned it out, maybe, just maybe, the mythical "god of lakes and waters" played a role. According to native legend, the northwest corner of Lake Superior had long been home to the "god of lakes and waters," also known as Manitou Niba Nibas. In a sworn statement before two judges of the Court of the King's Bench in Montreal on November 13, 1813, Venant St. Germain, a veteran voyageur for the North West Company, claimed that just after sunset on May 13, 1782, he and four others saw a strange "merman" near Pie Island, in the vicinity of Thunder Bay, Lake Superior. His party was camping for the night on the island. After coming ashore from setting some fish nets in the hope of getting a good breakfast of fresh trout, they were startled by an incredible creature. St. Germain later testified he saw "an animal in the water which appeared to have the upper part of its body above the waist formed exactly like that of a human being. It had half its body out of the water and the novelty of so extraordinary a spectacle excited his attention and led him to examine it carefully. The body of the animal seemed to be about the size of a child of seven or eight years of age with one of its arms extended and elevated in the air. The hand appeared to have the exposed fingers exactly similar to that of a man." St. Germain continued that he " ... distinctly saw the features of the countenance which bore an exact resemblance to those of the human face. The eyes were extremely brilliant; the nose small but handsomely shaped; the mouth proportional to the rest of the face; the complexion of brownish hue, the ears well formed and corresponding to the other parts of the figure."

For three or four minutes the beast glared at the voyageur and his companions as they, mouths agape, stared back. Finally St. Germain put his musket to shoulder to shoot, but an old Indian woman who was traveling with them pushed it away, cautioning him that this was the infamous "god of lakes and waters." Ominously, she also related that since all had seen it, they were all doomed. There was no escape from its terrible vengeance.

As soon as the woman finished her warning, the creature sank back into the depths and was seen no more. When they splashed ashore the old woman refused to walk the beach back to camp, instead climbing a steep bank and traveling through the woods. She was afraid Manitou Niba Nibas would send waves to wash her out into the lake where she would surely drown.

That night a tremendous storm pummeled the island. Huge trees toppled to the ground and mountainous waves swept the beach. The native woman was right. Manitou Niba Nibas did come for them. Her timing was just off. St. Germain and his companions survived the storm but spooked by the woman's warning knew it was the result of seeing the reclusive god. In his later deposition, St. Germain also claimed other voyageurs had seen the creature afterward in the same area of the lake.

Are the lighthouse curse and Manitou Niba Nibas related? Did building the light on lonely Talbot Island somehow offend the god, resulting in the death of the three keepers? Or did the men see the merman, therefore sealing their own death? And what of the mysterious ghost of the woman with the long white hair that the fisherman reported? Is it the ghost of Mrs. Lamphier, either still keeping her long lonely vigil over her dead husband or is she searching vainly for his grave, somehow unaware that he is buried on nearby Bowman Island?[3]

The Spirit of Rock of Ages

Rock of Ages Lighthouse is roughly five miles off the southwest tip of Lake Superior's Isle Royale, Michigan. Started in 1907 and finished in 1910, the eight-story-high tower marks the treacherous Rock of Ages Reef, the scene of three major shipwrecks. Two of the wrecks, the side-wheeler *Cumberland* in 1877 and propeller *Henry Chisholm* in 1898, perished before the light was built. The third, the steamer *George M. Cox* occurred in 1933. The lighthouse keeper played a major role in rescuing 121 passengers and crew from the stricken *Cox.*

The original second order Fresnel lens flashed a 940,000 candle power light visible for 29 miles in clear weather. It is said the light was visible over 50 miles, if conditions were just right! It was one of the most powerful lights on the Great Lakes. Because of its isolation, construction was considered a major engineering feat.

The light was automated in 1978. No longer did men polish the lens, paint the tower and provide the day-to-day tender loving care that the light deserved. Now it was just a cold, heartless machine that flicked the beam on at dusk and off at dawn. It

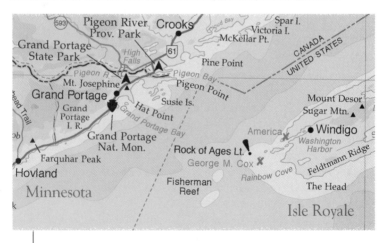

Rock of Ages Lighthouse sits to the west-southwest of Isle Royale.

28

Rock of Ages Light. UNITED STATES COAST GUARD

certainly wasn't the same. The Fresnel lens was removed in 1985 and taken to the Isle Royale National Park Windigo Ranger Station for display. It was replaced by a 300mm (12-inch diameter) Lucite lens. The old keepers would have wept!

Rock of Ages Light was always considered remote duty and it took a special breed of man to survive the isolation and loneliness. By any measure, it is a forlorn and melancholy place. There was no house as such. The men lived in the tower, mostly on the fourth level. The reefs are so dangerous that the lighthouse tenders could not safely approach the light and all supplies had to be landed by small boat, then hoisted up to the tower by a crane. Many of the old keepers grew to enjoy their duty at the light. It could be that at least one of them never really left. One of the keepers spent six years at the light, only leaving when he died. Perhaps it is his spirit that still haunts the tower.

In 1972, one of the Coast Guardsmen who was stationed at the light reported that it was haunted. He claimed the generator room door would open and close by itself, even when it was locked!

29

When left open it would, "close of its own volition," even though it had very stiff hinges. The door was heavy steel and moving it at any time took effort. It certainly wasn't being affected by any gust of air. He said that others on his crew saw the same phenomenon but were reluctant to speak about it. Could it be the ghost of the dead keeper out to help his Coast Guard buddies, or was the keeper still on his rounds to make certain his light is still shining?[4]

Stannard Rock Light Again

Lake Superior's Stannard Rock Light is located 44 miles north of Marquette, Michigan. During the period it was manned, 1882-1961, it was known as the "loneliest place in America." It was the most isolated lighthouse in North America.

The full story of its construction and eventual abandonment is told in my book, *Haunted Lakes, Great Lakes Maritime Ghost Stories, Superstitions and Sea Serpents,* the predecessor to this volume. In short, though, Stannard Rock Light was built in 1882 to mark a dangerous shoal perilously close to the shipping lanes. The rock tower stands a full 110 feet high and originally held a second order Fresnel lens, one of the largest on the Great Lakes. During the process of automating the light in 1961, a gas explosion killed one man and injured three. Since the original publication of *Haunted Lakes* in 1997, other tales of supernatural activity at the light have been discovered.

In 1993, the 180-foot Coast Guard buoy tender *Sundew* sent a four-man crew to the lighthouse to service the automated equipment. After the work crew landed, the weather deteriorated and the men could not safely be recovered. The area around Stannard Rock is filled with reefs, preventing the big tender from coming directly alongside the concrete lighthouse pier. Normal procedure was for the tender to lay off the light and send the service crew to the light in a small boat known as a rigid hull inflatable (RHI). That was the procedure followed in this instance.

When the weather turned bad, the Coast Guardsman in charge of the crew discussed the situation with the *Sundew* by hand radio and agreed not to tempt fate by fighting the waves in the RHI. They would remain overnight at the light. With only their leftover lunches, they volunteered to "crash" at the light.

The night passed quietly, at least for those on the *Sundew.* The big tender tugged at her anchor as the waves knocked her about a bit, but otherwise all was normal. The next morning, the seas calmed and the RHI ran into the light and picked up the marooned men. One of the crew on *Sundew* watched when they returned to the ship. "… they were literally gray in the face when I saw them on the mess deck. (Unidentified), a swarthy fellow with a clipper ship tattooed on his forearm, swore, along with the others, they would never go back." As the hungry sailors tore into the typical good Coast Guard breakfast, they eagerly related what happened.

"All night long, someone was running up and down the stairs." The men had slept on the fourth or fifth levels, the old crew quarters. "The trash cans we brought with us were kicked and thrown around the whole night!" None of the four men was aware of the 1961 explosion and resulting ghost stories. They learned the hard way – first hand! Was it the ghost of the Coast Guardsman killed in the 1961 explosion, or the spirit of one of the old civilian lightkeepers that they heard?

The *Sundew* had another strange encounter with Stannard Rock. The tender was anchored off the light waiting out weather for a day and a half. These 180 class ships are great sea vessels, but they *do* roll, and the crew was getting very tired of the motion. In a bit of horseplay, one of young sailors photocopied a picture of the sea god Neptune, wrote the name of one of the ship's old chiefs on it and tacked it on the ship's bulletin board. The crusty old chief didn't take the kidding easily and hauled the culprit to the mess deck where he was chewed out as only a chief can do! The sailor was told that he had insulted the great sea god and must apologize for his transgressions immediately. The miscreant was made to go up to the open buoy deck, kneel, beg Neptune

Stannard Rock Light. UNITED STATES COAST GUARD

31

for forgiveness and then throw the offending picture overboard. Virtually the entire crew watched the mysterious ceremony with due gravity. The salt-stained old chief must have had a special relationship with Neptune, because within an hour the lake surface calmed to glass![5]

Grandfather's Ghost

There was a time before all the lighthouses were automated when keeping the light was a family affair. The responsibility was not taken lightly and everyone pitched in when the situation demanded. This story was related to me some years ago by a little gray haired old lady. I obviously can't vouch for its veracity, but the woman who told it certainly believed it happened, As you can see, she told it in a very straight forward manner. I did very little editing. It is a strange tale, but after all is said and done, who are we to doubt it?

"I guess I was a lighthouse brat. Father was a keeper and so was grandfather, so I grew up with the old service, before the Coast Guard took over in the '40s. It was a tremendous experience. Grandfather kept the light at the island just down the coast while father had the lighthouse at the point. I used to visit back and forth. The long summer days at the island with grandfather and grandmother were wonderful. The sea gulls always used to welcome me as I landed on the little dock, diving and wheeling away again and again. I remember the sweet aroma of the apple pies grandmother baked and set to cool on the kitchen window sill. The apples came from their own small orchard of a dozen trees or so just on the west end of the island. Those were the best apples. I never knew what variety they were but they were the sweetest I've ever eaten. Grandfather had a small sailboat and on special days would take me out to hand line for lake trout.

"Of course I spent most of my time with my parents at the point. We were too far from town for me to go to school, so mother taught me at home. That wasn't as bad as it sounds, not having the other children to play with, I mean. The big white kitchen table was my desk and she had the same books they used in town. And mother was awfully smart and had a real knack for explaining things. I thought she was a good teacher. And it was nice to get hot cookies as they came out of the oven, too! Kids in town didn't get that! By high school time, though, I went to town and boarded with a local family during the school year. I made a lot of friends there, but really missed being home with my lighthouse.

"But this isn't about me. Let me tell you about my grandfather. It's a strange story and I will tell it as I remember it. I never told this to anyone else before and it happened a long time ago, so if I skip around or the details are foggy, please forgive me.

"One November we had a terrible storm come through. The kind father always called a hell-banger. Mountain high seas and screaming winds really tore at us. A couple of our big oak trees were knocked over and our chicken coop completely blew away. We never found it or the chickens. Grandmother was visiting with us so grandfather was alone at the island. I don't remember where his assistant was off to; in any case, he was gone.

"That night grandfather's light never came on. The tower was dark! Normally we could see its flash off in the distance from our tower. Sometimes it would reflect off the clouds in a really eerie fashion. Later, when the storm really hit, we couldn't hardly see anything, let alone grandfather's light. It was black as sin! During the night an old wood steamer smashed right into the reef just off shore from grandfather's island. About half the crew made it to shore in their lifeboat. The rest died in the wreck.

"The men that made it to the beach looked up and saw the dark lamp room and they were mad as hell. They figured the keeper was drunk or something, thinking if the light was on, they would not have hit the rocks.

"In any case, they went to the house and found it empty. A couple of oil lanterns were burning, but no one was there. They then went to the tower. Part way up the stairs they found grandfather laying on the steps stone-cold dead. Apparently his heart gave out on his way up to the lamp room.

"The strange thing was just about dusk, around when we later thought grandfather must have died, we were having supper and grandmother looked up and gasped, 'He's dead, I know it!' She started to cry and ran from the table. Mother and father tried to console her, but she wouldn't listen to their words. She cried all night. I didn't know what to do, so I cried, too.

"After we found out what happened at the island it all made sense. Anyway, within a year grandmother died, too. She just kind of pined away – didn't eat, didn't sleep, mostly just sat in the big corner chair and stared. We buried her next to grandfather in the little island cemetery. The service sent a new keeper to take his place and he was a good man, but it wasn't the same.

"A couple of years later mother died. They said it was consumption, but I don't think the doctors really knew what was the cause. She just took sick and in a couple of weeks passed away. We buried her on the island, too.

"Losing mother was tough on father. But he still had me. Really we had each other. In a way it was very ideal. I took over running the house, buying the food, cooking and cleaning, trying to take mother's place. I really had to grow up in a hurry and tried my very best.

"We had a great assistant keeper. I know during the time right after Mom's passing he was really doing more than he was supposed to, taking over some of Dad's work while we kind of sorted things out. In early fall the assistant was killed in a tragic accident. He had taken the sailboat out to do a little fishing and best anyone can guess lost his attention and the boom struck him in the head hard enough to knock him out and into the water. The boat drifted ashore the next day. His body was found a week later with the back of his head all bashed in.

"It was just afterwards the second storm came. Like the one Grandfather died in, it was a hell-banger too. For weeks following it, the papers were filled with stories of ships wrecked and sailors drowned. They didn't find some of the bodies until the spring.

"The night when the storm was at its peak, Father was terribly ill with a fever, delirious mostly. I thought for a while I was going to lose him, too. Of course, the service still had not sent a new assistant yet. It was just Father and me against that terrible storm.

"With Father sick in bed, I knew it was up to me to get the lamp lit and make sure it stayed burning. The tower was 50 yards or so away from the house and just getting there was a fight. The winds were blasting so hard I was afraid I would be blown away, especially with my long dress. I remember I crawled on my hands and knees part of the way.

"When I finally reached the stone tower it was actually shaking from the force of the wind. I could feel the brick vibrating! Lord, did the wind shriek! I started up the steps. Part way up one of the small windows blew out sending shards of glass raining down the stairs. Some of it fell into my hair. I cut my fingers trying to get it out.

"I kept fighting my way up the stairs, worrying all the time about the ships on the lake that were depending on the light. I could even hear a captain saying, "Where is it, where is that light? I know it is here somewhere." No matter what, I had to get the lamp lit.

"When I crawled through the scuttle hatch and looked out at the lake, it was the wildest I have ever seen it. The waves were massive, the size of houses. When they hit the rocks below the spray flew high into the lamp room windows. It was just terrible! Up in the top of the tower it was really shaking. I was afraid it would fall over.

"All the time I spent in lighthouses I had never lit the lamp. Both Grandfather and Father wouldn't let me touch it. Both said it was their special responsibility and no one else could do it. But now it was up to me. I tried to recall exactly what they did. Carefully I removed the white linen dust cover from the lens. Then I opened the tiny oil faucet and waited the required 10 minutes. Father always described what he was doing, so I remember that. Ten minutes, not more or less. I had no watch so I had to guess the time. The lamp had a little brass damper tube device that had to be set just so on a set of brass pins. Then the glass chimney was raised up a little bit. The wick had been trimmed that morning when Father extinguished the light, so it was all ready. I had to light the wick, then adjust the chimney and wick height carefully and then slowly regulate the damper as I brought the flame up to full brightness.

"I couldn't do it! My hands shook so much I kept knocking the plunger off the pins or twisted the wick down instead of up and put it out. Once I hit the chimney with my hand so hard I was sure I broke it. I don't know how many times I tried to get it going and just couldn't do it. Tears were welling up in my eyes and I couldn't see, but I kept trying to light it. I was in a panic!

"I was failing. Some poor ship and crew would wreck and men would die because of me! Suddenly I heard Grandfather's soft voice behind me. 'Slow down girl, you can do it. Those sailors depend on you.' Despite the wind, I clearly heard him. Turning quickly, I saw my grandfather standing right behind me. I should have been scared. I mean, he had been dead and in the ground for years. Instead, I only felt very calm and peaceful. There was nothing misty about him either. He was as solid as I am. His blue eyes still sparkled like always. He looked right at me and said, 'I failed once, but not again. Just take your time. You watched me do it enough. You remember how.' Then it was easy, just like I had done it a thousand times before. When I turned back, Grandfather was gone.

"That storm blew for two more days. Just like the earlier one, it left many ships wrecked and crews drowned. But not off our light, thanks to my grandfather. Father started getting better the next day. I had to keep the light for several days until he was strong enough to take over again. He was very proud of me for being the lightkeeper. However, I never did say anything to him about what really happened that night.

"About a week later the new assistant showed up. Lord he was handsome! He looked just like Grandfather in the old wedding picture that always stood on their mantel. Tall, blue eyes. Oh, he was a real lady killer. I was smitten from the very first. I married him three years later. Father retired soon after and we stayed on at the light, the new keeper and his child bride. I never saw Grandfather again. But I never questioned what I saw and heard in the tower that night. It was Grandfather's ghost and he had come back to help."

Norman's Back - Pipe Island

Pipe Island is located north of the Detour Passage from Lake Huron to the St. Marys River. The shipping channel runs just to the west of the island and a light on the southwest corner helps to mark this critical spot. Sailors running the St. Marys River always look for Pipe Island.

Pipe Island Light also has the reputation of being haunted. Although little is known of the nature of the spirit, it seems to speculatively center on Norman Hawkins, one of the early keepers. It was said he was despondent over his only son's death in a hunting accident and as a result late one night he committed suicide, although he lingered for days before finally succumbing. Subsequent keepers claim to have seen his ghost, in one instance standing in a lighthouse doorway clad in dripping oilskins.

Others have reported unexplained poltergeist activity in the house, such as slamming doors, unscrewing light bulbs, moving fire wood, running water taps, all actions without explanation or cause. Where the truth is, of course, is unknown. But the signs would seem to say, "Norman's Back."[6]

Pipe Island Lighthouse in the St. Marys River is another of the ghostly lights. AUTHOR'S COLLECTION

Raspberry Island

Where are the ghosts? For an area as well populated with lighthouses as Lake Superior's Apostle Islands, there should be spirits everywhere. Strangely, apparently there are not. There are seven lighthouses in the Apostle Island group: La Pointe (1857), Michigan Island (1857), Raspberry Island (1862), Outer Island (1874), Sand Island (1882), Devils Island (1891) and Chequamegon Point (1897). Given this large number of potential haunting sites, the lack of reported ghost stories is amazing.

The Apostle Island lighthouses served the important objective of guiding ships safely through and around the islands. When the first iron ore docks in Ashland, Wisconsin, opened in 1886, the lights assumed a new value. Although Ashland never rivaled Duluth, Minnesota, as a major shipping point, in 1906 it recorded 2,000 vessel arrivals and departures. The efficient operation of the Apostle Island lights was obviously important to the city and overall Lake Superior commerce.

One of the oldest of the Apostle Island lights is at Raspberry Island. Although the site for the lighthouse was selected in 1859, it was the spring of 1863 before the light was first exhibited. Through the years many improvements were made, including a new fog signal, boat houses and living quarters. Today the National Park Service runs a very active interpretative program at the lighthouse. An actor plays the role of an assistant keeper, circa 1923, and for the four months of the summer season, he shows visitors what it was like to live and work on the lonely island.

There are two instances of possible haunting at Raspberry Island. In the first, a National Park volunteer was up in the tower after work hours enjoying the solitude and playing her flute when the door to the catwalk inexplicably slammed shut, the latch sliding into the catch, locking her out. She remained trapped on the narrow gallery until a passerby saw her plight, climbed the tower and opened the door. Was it just the wind, or something else? Considering the weight of the door, an errant gust of wind would seem most unusual.

Some years later a volunteer keeper was taking a tourist through the house when another strange incident occurred. The day was cold and rainy, one of those days when it is best just to stay inside out of the weather. On days like these, tourist traffic to the island is virtually nil. As the guide was escorting his lone visitor through the house, the man asked if the keeper had his children on the island with him. The keeper replied that, while he was married, his wife was on the mainland and they had no children and to his knowledge none were on the island. The tourist commented that he could hear children playing outside. The keeper listened but heard nothing. Later the visitor commented that although most of the words the children were yelling were too soft for him to clearly hear, one did sound like "mutter." In German this translates as, "mother." Many of the old keepers were of German ancestry. Could there be a bizarre connection between the soft cries of an unseen child on a dismal rainy day and perhaps another dimension?

The Ghostly Girl of Tawas Light

Lighthouse ghosts are not only the spirits of gray-bearded old keepers. Sometimes they can be the shades of others who experienced both joy and sorrow at the lights. The ghostly girl at Tawas Point Light, Michigan, on the Lake Huron shore, is a fine example of the latter variety.

The first lighthouse at Tawas Point, a rubble tower similar to the one at Old Presque Isle Light just 70 miles to the north, was operational in 1853. By the early 1870s, the point had shifted enough that a new light was needed and the present lighthouse was constructed as the result. The brick tower stands 67 feet high, giving the fourth order Fresnel lens a focal plane 70 feet above the lake. A two-story brick keeper's house is attached.

Pinning down the reason for a ghost is always the purest

Tawas Point Lighthouse. AUTHOR'S COLLECTION

The concrete steps where the little girl in pink was sitting. AUTHOR'S COLLECTION.

conjecture. In this instance, it seems that a young girl, thought to be the daughter of the lightkeeper, died in one of the upstairs bedrooms around the turn of the century. Apparently the death was caused by pneumonia. Old-timers say her spirit has haunted the old light ever since. She isn't confined to the building, but also has been seen on the grounds around the lighthouse.

One of the more modern stories involves the wife of the Coast Guard officer-in-charge of the station. Up until very recently, the lighthouse was an active part of the Tawas Coast Guard Station. Before the new officer-in-charge and his wife moved into their quarters, they were staying in a camper trailer parked near the lighthouse. It was a pleasant spring morning and since the Coast Guard station is closed to the public, the grounds were deserted. The wife was sitting at a picnic table enjoying her coffee, when to her surprise, she noticed a young girl in a pink gown sitting on the stone steps at the rear of the lighthouse. The little girl was crying. The woman thought this was very odd and she walked over and asked the girl where she was from and what she was doing? The girl looked up at her for a long moment and then ran through the back door and into the lighthouse. Since the door was locked with a padlock, this was impossible! Startled, the woman ran back to the

The window at upper left of the Tawas Point Lighthouse building is said to have been the little girl's bedroom. Witnesses claim to have seen her looking out. Author's Collection.

camper and got her husband. Between them, they couldn't figure out what had happened. All the doors were locked as were the windows. When the husband searched the building, no evidence of the little girl was found.

There have been other encounters with the mysterious little girl. She has been sighted looking forlornly out of her top floor bedroom window. Reportedly this was the room she was in when she died. She has also been seen peering out of the upstairs windows at the rear of the house. Is she looking for playmates who will never come? Why is she trapped at the lighthouse at all? Why didn't she "pass over?"

It is reported that in 1998, a group of Coast Guardsmen had another brush with the little ghost. The officer-in-charge of the station, engineering officer and two Coast Guard engineers from Coast Guard Group Detroit were in the lighthouse basement checking the facility when they heard a little girl's voice outside. It sounded as if she was playing, laughing and carrying-on the way children do. Finding this odd, since they knew there were no children in the area, the men went back outside to see what was going on. They discovered there was no one around the light! As far as they could see, they were alone. They must have been mistaken. The men went back to the basement to finish their work. As soon as they reached the basement, they heard the little girl again. One of the men was so rattled by the unearthly experience, he refused to ever enter the lighthouse again! The same man was involved as a local scout leader and when he brought his group to tour the lighthouse, he stood outside in the bright sunshine, unwilling to set foot in the building.

Perhaps there are more wandering ghosts at Tawas Point than just the little girl in pink. Just to the northwest of the light is the old Tawas Coast Guard Station. A new, "state-of-the-art" Coast Guard Station was built across the road, so the old one is currently abandoned. The original station was built by the U.S. Life-Saving Service in 1876. There are stories of bizarre events happening in the old station house. One evening after the men had moved to the new station, the Search and Rescue (SAR) alarm in the old station house suddenly blared to life as if to summon the crew to a rescue. Considering that there was no electrical power to the building, this was most remarkable! It continued to sound until station men came to see what was going on, when it stopped as mysteriously as it started. This wasn't the only odd happening in the building. On previous occasions, Coast Guardsmen working on the ground floor of the building clearly heard people moving about and talking on the upper floor. In the days of the old lifesaving crews, this was where the men had their bunks and lockers. When they checked,

The Tawas Point Coast Guard Station. AUTHOR'S COLLECTION.

the room was empty – of the living! After a while, they didn't bother to look anymore. It was just part of the old lifeboat station.[7]

Hearing the sounds of the spirits of old surfman (for want of a better description) in the second floor of old Life-Saving Stations isn't all that unusual. Just as all lighthouses seem to be haunted, so, too, all Life-Saving Stations. Similar tales have come from the Hammond's Bay station on Lake Huron and both South and North Manitou Island stations on Lake Michigan. In addition, the surfboat from Point aux Barques Station on Lake Huron has also supposedly been seen again (see *Haunted Lakes,* pages 108-110).

The Haunts of Eagle Harbor Light

The ghosts at Eagle Harbor Lighthouse are more difficult to identify than the shades in an "average" haunted lighthouse. Some ghosts are heard and seen. Others only manifest themselves as flitting shadows dancing across a room, or perhaps projecting a feeling of deep dread or fear. They do not seem to link to any particular time, event or person. Nonetheless, from all accounts spirits do occupy the old light station. At least one person sensitive to spirits visited the lighthouse and felt their chilling presence.

The first lighthouse at Eagle Harbor, Michigan, was completed in 1851, with the purpose of helping guide vessels working in the great Keweenaw copper boom. Like most of the early lighthouse construction, it was built so poorly that a new lighthouse was built in 1870 to replace it. Other than the fog horn building, there are two frame houses on the grounds, one white and one brown. Both were built in the 1940s and moved to the light station from the old Coast Guard station across the harbor when it was closed.

One of the Coast Guardsmen stationed at the lighthouse in the 1970s remembered numerous strange occurrences. Both the brick lighthouse building and the white house nearby are considered haunted. Living in the lighthouse, he remembered mysterious noises coming from the second floor bedroom, sounding like furniture was being moved around. Heavy footsteps echoed across the hardwood floor. The light switch at the base of the tower turned on and off of its own accord on numerous occasions. He also saw an eerie light coming through from the crack under the first floor tower door. When he would open the door, the light would always disappear. The Coast Guardsman complained to the District Office in Cleveland about the weird goings on, but to no avail. Since ghosts did not exist in the Coast Guard, there can't be any complaints about them!

The Eagle Harbor Lighthouse is supposedly home to things that "go bump in the night." AUTHOR'S COLLECTION.

Once an overnight guest staying in the lighthouse claimed to have seen a ghost in the bedroom late at night. The specter was that of a man in a flannel shirt, but he had no face. The witness was badly shaken by the experience and vowed never to return to the lighthouse.

After the Coast Guardsman put up with the ghostly antics for a year, the white house became vacant and he moved into it in an effort to flee the spirits. Moving was a bad decision. If anything, this house was even more haunted. In mid-winter he would be awakened by weird voices in his bedroom. They seemed to come from everywhere and yet nowhere. He heard heavy footsteps tramping around on the first floor at night after he had retired to his upstairs bedroom. The footsteps would move across the hardwood floor, slowly clump up the stairs to the second floor, move down the hall and stop at the entrance to his bedroom. By the time the steps reached his door, the Coast Guardsman was terrified and covered with sweat. After a few long minutes the steps would start again but now moving across his ceiling! He remembered that without explanation weird things would happen in the house, bizarre noises, lights turning on and off, doors opening and closing, all activities reminiscent of invisible occupants still "living" in their houses.

When the brown house became vacant, the Coast Guardsman moved into it. Anything was better than what he was putting up within the white house. To his relief, he was the only occupant. Nothing went "bump in the night," no footsteps echoed in empty halls or other ghostly manifestations happened. There were no mysterious lights or voices floating on the air. By contrast, the families that moved into the lighthouse and white house were occasionally bedeviled by the same mysterious events as he had been.[8]

While to this writer's knowledge no one has ever conducted a séance to identify the spirits, a good guess, however, for the lighthouse ghost might be that of Stephen Cocking, lightkeeper from September 21, 1877, through November 21, 1889. He is the only keeper recorded as having died at the light. Many of the old keepers became very attached to their lights. Perhaps Cocking was one of these dedicated men who just refused to "cross over the final bar." Why spirits should be in the house is unknown.

CHAPTER 2

Ghost Ships

Ghost ships continue to be part of the fabric of Great Lakes legend and lore. There are stories of persistent ghost ships like the *Bannockburn* and *Chicora,* seen again and again by lake sailors down through the years. Tales of these vessels and others are told in the original *Haunted Lakes.* However, there are many more yarns of phantom ships and the crews that man them.

The *Altadoc,* Again!

A terrific storm on December 7-9, 1927, wrecked five steel ships on Lake Superior. Northwest winds screamed across the lake in excess of 70 mph and heavy snow blotted out visibility. Temperatures fell to 19 degrees below zero, causing a weighty ice to coat the vessels. Ships and their crews on the lake took a terrible beating.

The 376-foot steamer *E. W. Oglebay,* upbound light on Lake Superior from Sault Ste. Marie for Fort William, Ontario, was driven ashore at Shot Point, east of Marquette, Michigan. Her crew was rescued by the Coast Guard station at Marquette. At the same time *Oglebay* was crunching ashore, the 365-foot Canadian steamer *Altadoc,* also bound for Fort William, was battling the storm in mid-lake. As a result of the smashing seas, she lost her rudder and was unable to steer. Forced into the trough of the waves, the northwest storm drove her relentlessly down for the deadly rock coast of the Keweenaw Peninsula. All through the dark night the helpless steamer rolled and plunged, waiting anxiously for the screech of her steel hull on rock that would soon come. At 7 a.m.

The Altadoc *ashore at Keweenaw Point.* AUTHOR'S COLLECTION

the crew waited no longer, the steamer ground hard into the Keweenaw rocks north of Copper Harbor. Eventually the men were rescued by the Eagle Harbor Coast Guard lifeboat. The steamer proved to be a total loss and was finally cut for scrap during World War II.

Another deadly drama was unfolding northwest of Isle Royale. The 250-foot Canada Steamship Lines vessel *Kamloops* had fought her way up from the Soo. It was a tough run and it looked like she would make it, then disaster struck! Apparently she lost her stack or suffered some kind of engine breakdown and fell into the trough of the waves. There she capsized and sank. Some of her crew were able to escape in a lifeboat and reach Isle Royale, only to freeze to death on the deserted island. In the spring, searchers found some of them in grotesque postures of death. The fate of the ship remained a mystery until 50 years later, when the hull was discovered off the island's Twelve O'clock Point.

Two other vessels fared better. The 349-foot steamer *Martian* stranded hard on Hare Island near Thunder Cape and the 252-foot *Lambton* went ashore in Whitefish Bay. Both of these vessels were later recovered.

This was the situation following the devastating storm. Now events jump forward to 1932, five years after the *Altadoc* died on the rocks of the Keweenaw. A local fisherman in a small boat is working his way slowly up the coast. The lake is rough, but not storm tossed, and thick snow squalls sweep over the water. Under

46

such conditions good navigation is imperative to keep clear of the many rocks, not to mention being able to get back home.

Without warning, a wall of darkness appeared directly in front of him! Thinking, "What the hell?" he turned hard to port and swung away from the thing – whatever it was. As the snow lightened, he saw it was a ship and a big steel one at that, about several hundred yards ahead. It looked to be dead in the water and drifting. It was also moving too fast for the winds he was in. Her motion was all wrong, too. She was far too lively, too much action to her. It was as if an invisible gale were pushing the ship through unseen waves. The name *Altadoc* stood out clearly on her bow.

Stunned, the fisherman watched in awe as the big ship moved quickly and inexorably across his bow until it again smashed soundlessly on the rocky beach. A fast moving snow squall blotted out the wrecked ship in a wall of white. The man knew what he had seen. The *Altadoc* was a ghost ship and such phantoms brought no good to anyone. His nets would wait until tomorrow. He came about and went home as fast as he could.

He had just finished making his boat fast to the dock when the first gusts of a vicious northwester blasted across the lake. Had he continued to pull his nets, he would have been in the middle of it and he knew it was a ship-killer. When his wife asked why he was back so soon and where the fish were, he told her nothing of the *Altadoc,* complaining only of the weather.[9]

Hats in the Water

Silently they bobbed in the calm water. There were 30 or 40 of them in all. They weren't keeping any special formation, just drifting around at the whim of wind and current. When the man looked closer, he saw they were hats, some from sailors and the rest from soldiers. How did they end up on this lonely stretch of Lake Ontario beach? Later he discovered they were all that was left of His Majesty's Ship *Ontario,* the most powerful warship on Lake Ontario.

During the Revolutionary War, the British maintained a strong naval force on the Great Lakes. HMS *Ontario* was an important part of the battle fleet. The 86-foot-long sloop was launched at Carleton Island, Lake Ontario, on May 10, 1780. Armed with 16 6-pound and six 4-pound cannons, the ship was strong enough to give a good account of herself in a battle with any American vessel.

Toward the end of October 1780, a bare five months after her launching, she sailed from Niagara bound for the British fort at

Oswego. Aboard were a large number of British soldiers along with their supplies. A small number of women and children accompanied the troops. Supposedly, *Ontario* also carried a large payroll in gold and silver coin.

On Halloween night a shrieking west gale tore down the length of Lake Ontario, building up tremendous waves. When the weather cleared, *Ontario* and her human cargo were gone. The death list included 70 sailors and soldiers, several Native American people plus four other women and five children.

The caps discovered by settlers along the south shore were, other than a couple of hatch covers, virtually all the wreckage there was. Not a single body of the passengers or crew was ever reported recovered.

Treasure hunters have looked hard for the wreck, based on the rumored gold and silver cargo, but to date, all have come up empty handed. The *Ontario* is another mystery that the lake keeps.

Two centuries ago people were more superstitious than they are today, or at least that is our smug belief. In the depths of a cold fall, when slate grey clouds sweep over the lake and the night is dark and gloomy, old-timers claim the warship can be seen again. They see the decks crowded by red-coated soldiers and yards heavy with sailors trying desperately to fist in flapping sails as the ship plunges wildly in the mounting seas. The old-tars believe she is doomed to repeat her death struggle again and again. The apparition never lingers long, perhaps for half a minute or so. In a blink the *Ontario* is gone, back to wherever ghost ships spend their days.[10]

The *Eastland* Disaster

When the steamer *Eastland* capsized in her Chicago slip on Saturday, July 24, 1915, with the loss of 844 lives, it was the greatest maritime disaster in the Great Lakes. The day was supposed to be the annual Western Electric Company picnic to Michigan City, Indiana. To transport the 7,500 employees, friends and family members, the company chartered four steamers, the *Eastland, Theodore Roosevelt, Missouri* and *City of South Haven*. All the steamers were moored in the Chicago River between the Clark Street and LaSalle Street bridges. Since *Eastland* and *Theodore Roosevelt* were the newest ships, most employees were anxious to travel aboard them, instead of the other steamers.

The *Eastland* was built in 1903 for passenger and fruit hauling across Lake Michigan between Chicago and South Haven, Michigan. Later she cruised between Cleveland and Cedar Point,

The steamer Eastland, *in happier days.* AUTHOR'S COLLECTION

Ohio. For the 1915 season she was owned by the St. Joseph-Chicago Line. Always known as a fast ship, she also had a well known tendency to roll.

At 6:40 a.m. passengers began to board *Eastland*. Almost immediately she began to list to starboard, toward the dock. Doubtless this was due to the crush of passengers rushing aboard to secure the best viewing locations for the trip down the river. Most of the passengers had not yet spread out throughout the ship. Nevertheless, the chief engineer was able to flood the port ballast tanks to straighten her out. At 6:51 a.m. she was again level.

Two minutes later, the *Eastland* lurched 10 degrees to port, which caused the engineer to fill her starboard tanks to again level her. At 7:10 a.m. she resumed to her port list, causing the engineer to pump out her port tanks in an effort to balance her, but not before she had reached a 15-degree list. Eventually the engineer was able to briefly level the ship, before it lurched back to a 20-degree port list. At this point water began to flood through the lower port side view ports. At 7:28 a.m. the list reached 45 degrees. Now the real danger was recognized by everyone, but it was too late to take remedial action. The big steamer gently continued to roll to port, snapping her mooring lines one by one, eventually ending up with its starboard side out of the water. Lucky passengers found themselves standing on the steel hull. Many others were desperately thrashing in the river.

Survivors crowded the steamer's hull. AUTHOR'S COLLECTION

An observer remembers that horrible scene. "I shall never be able to forget what I saw. People were struggling in the water, clustered so thickly that they literally covered the surface of the river. A few were swimming; the rest were floundering about, some clinging to a life raft that had floated free, others clutching at anything they could reach – bits of wood, at each other, grabbing each other, pulling each other down and screaming! The screaming was the most horrible of all!"

Boats in the river came as fast as possible to help the victims. People ashore threw planks, wood crates and anything else that would float into the water. However, hundreds of men, women and children were hopelessly trapped in the hull!

The view ports were too small for any of the people trapped inside to escape through so crews from rescue boats cut holes into the side of the vessel to provide access. People caught inside screamed in terror. Cutting the holes was a slow process and by the time the crews made it through the hull, many had drowned. After making several trips into the flooded interior, it was said that one of the rescuers went mad! For days afterward, the rescuers worked at the grisly task of hauling bodies out of the hull and fishing them from the river.

An immediate problem was where to lay out the bodies. Several locations were used. One of the larger ones was the Second

Regiment Armory on Washington Boulevard. Row upon row of corpses lined the large drill floor. When all of the victims were counted, 844 people were dead, 841 passengers, two crewmen and one rescuer. Entire families were wiped out. Identification of the bodies was sometimes difficult when no one knew the dead. One source points out that more passengers were killed on the *Eastland* (841), than were killed on the *Titanic* (694). The total for the *Titanic* of 1,532 was reached only when the crew was included.

Why exactly the *Eastland* capsized has never been answered to complete satisfaction. It is clear she was top-heavy and had a reputation as being an unsteady ship. By design, her 265-foot length and 38.2-foot beam would have caused stability problems,

The scope of the disaster was incredible. AUTHOR'S COLLECTION

The wrecking tug Favorite *worked to raise the Eastland.* AUTHOR'S COLLECTION

which to a certain extent could be corrected by altering the water ballast. There were other factors. Prior to the 1915 season, two inches of concrete were poured over her decks to keep the wood planking from rotting. This added to her top-heaviness. Passengers preferred to ride on her upper decks for the better view, which further increased stability problems. In a way, the *Titanic* also contributed to the loss of the *Eastland*. After *Titanic*'s loss in 1912, there was a frantic rush to add sufficient lifeboats to passenger vessels to assure all passengers could be provided with space. The heavy lifeboats were added to her upper decks, further decreasing stability. The ship's capacity had also recently been increased from 2,000 to 2,500 passengers.

The official cause of loss was found by the courts to be the engineer failing to fill the water ballast tanks correctly. Of course the courts determining the cause of a maritime loss is in itself absurd.

The *Eastland* was refloated on August 14, 1915, and was an unwanted ship for four years. No one wanted a ship with her unsavory past. Finally, she was acquired by the U.S. government for use as a Navy training ship. The hull was cut down and she was rebuilt as the USS *Wilmette*. For 31 years, the ship was used to train naval recruits. In 1948, she was finally scrapped in Chicago.

The previous is fact. What follows is something else, perhaps even "spiritual."

One historian claimed that the *Eastland* was always a hoodoo ship. Shortly after launching, she failed to meet her design specifications and many modifications were needed. She also had a propensity for breaking down at the height of the season, thus costing her owners lost revenue.

Throughout her career there were rumors of the ship being unsafe. At one point her owners reputedly offered a reward of $5,000 to anyone who could prove the charge. Although no one ever did, the rumors certainly affected business.

In the months and years after the disaster, there were claims that pedestrians walking the area between the Clark and LaSalle Street bridges heard cries of horror near the river bank. On bright sunny mornings other people reported hearing a sudden splash, followed by hundreds of screaming voices. When they looked, there were no ripples, just a smooth surface of water.

If there is any truth to the old sailors' tale that those areas of the lakes that suffered great calamities remain haunted by the spirits of the dead, then this small stretch of the Chicago River is indeed filled with ghosts.

Two of the buildings pressed into service as temporary morgues were the old Reid Murdock building, now the traffic court and the building that houses the Oprah Winfrey Studio. The tale goes that

The Eastland *was resurrected as the USS* Wilmette. AUTHOR'S COLLECTION

Eastland *victims lined up in a temporary morgue.* AUTHOR'S COLLECTION

workers and visitors in both buildings have reported unusual occurrences and sensations. Sometimes it's a cold spot or the soft sound of quiet weeping echoing in an empty room. Psychics claim that the overall impression of death and mourning is pervasive.

The Phantom Schooner of Death's Door

Death's Door Passage, or "Porte des Morts," as the early French explorers called it, is a notorious ship trap. A narrow channel beset by reefs and strong currents, it cuts directly through the Door Peninsula and is the quickest path from Green Bay into Lake Michigan. Although the full total may never be known, hundreds of vessels have wrecked on its deadly reefs. In one 1880 gale alone, 30 ships wrecked in the area!

As might be expected, there are numerous tales of phantom ships still running through the deadly gauntlet. These "Flying Dutchmen" have been seen by lighthouse keepers, fishermen, sailors and landsmen. All were amazed at the wonderful sight these old wind-wagons presented.

A classic sighting happened in the 1940s. A small cruiser with two couples aboard was running through the passage eastward for Gills Rock when they hit rough water. They had intended to make the trip during daylight but had delayed too long and then mounting winds and waves slowed them down so night overtook the boat before reaching Gills Rock. The moon was full, so visibility was very good.

The small boat periodically went from trough to crest as large waves passed beneath. One minute they were deep in the water unable to see anything, the next high enough to see for miles. While perched momentarily on one of the crests, the occupants were startled to see lights from a boat dead ahead. Their first thought was that it was the Washington Island ferry, but at the next crest they realized that it had three masts and all sails were set. The big schooner seemed to be heading toward Gills Rock, too. When the boat again climbed to the top of the crest a moment later, the schooner was gone. There was nothing there but an empty horizon. What had happened to the phantom ship?[11]

An Old Sailor's Tale

"Now you jess sit your ass still and listen to me. Jess listen a mite to an old sailor before he crosses the bar for the last time. My knowledge box is still free of fog and you needs to hear me out before settlin' on a sail'n' way a life."

The grizzled old mariner leaned back against the wall of the saloon, gently cradling his glass of whiskey in gnarled hands, and looked the young sailor in the eyes. Smoke from cheap cigars hung heavy in the stale air and raucous laughter rose and fell from the sailors packed against the bar. A piano player banged out a barely recognizable tune on an old upright and several men and variety girls were kicking up the sawdust on the small dance floor. It was Saturday night and everyone was having a good time. The youth strained to hear the ancient mariner's words.

"Before you was even an sparkle in your father's eyes, I was out on these here lakes sailing the old wind wagons, not one of the damned steam boats, but the old canvas backs! They took men to sail 'em, not a bunch of farm boys. Anyways, I'm about all used up now, been in too many gaggers and maybe too many bars but I don't believe that for a second. Ain't nuthin' wrong with a dram of good barley now and then or rollin' with the dollies either!

"Back in '90, I was crew'n on the old *Comrade*. We was being pulled by the steamer *Columbia*. Both were real buckets. It was tough to get a job sailin' then and the barge was the best I could do on such short notice, but I'll get to that. Anyways, we pulled out of Ashland town in mid-September with a load of ore bound for

The steamer Columbia *lost her tow, the schooner* Comrade. *RUTHERFORD B. HAYES LIBRARY*

Cleveland. The going was good until off the Keweenaw, when a big southwester' rolled into us. Damn, it was a black one, one of the worst I've seen. 'Course being on that old barge didn't help. Queer look'n' thing she was. Built her as a lumber hooker, then changed their minds and didn't drop the engine in. Put a couple of sticks on her and called her a schooner-barge. She war a barge all right, but ain't no schooner in her, no ways! She'd been rough-handled, too, and weren't in no good shape, I'll tell you! We was maybe 20 miles off entry when the hawser let go. The *Columbia* didn't come back for us. Don't blame 'em at all. The seas were really rolling too high for her to try to get us a new line. We tried to get some canvas on the sticks to steady her up, maybe even let us work back to behind the Apostles, but the stuff was all rotten and blew out as soon as we bent it on. There were eight of us and we just hung on. There weren't nuthin'' else we could do. We was rollin' so bad I was sure the sticks would come right out of her too. Them old high cabins on her jess caught the wind gusts somethin' awful. All the while we was jess drifting with the gale. Night came and it were darker than death's night to a feller what don't take no stock in the hereafter. After a bit, the mate came up and told us the water's getting up in the hold – must have split some oakum, from the way we was plunging in the waves. As the hours went by, the barge just squatted lower and lower in the water. Towards the end, the waves were

56

rolling right down the deck. We started to get the boat ready figuring it was time to leave her when the damn barge left us, jess dropping right away from under our feet! I must have got sucked down cause I remember everything being black, then breaking surface and looking around. I spotted the yawl a few yards away, swam to it and hung on.

"I hear another feller yelling over to my right, but I got no oars so all I can do is hang on. After a while I don't hear him no more so I guess he's gone.

"I don't know how long I drifted around, jest hanging on to that old yawl. It was a long time though. Finally the lake calmed to kind of a big oily swell. Then the fog set in. Thick and cold. I could see maybe 20 yards, hardly anything really. I was terrible cold, just froze to the bone. I don't care what time of year it is, the big lake is cold all the time.

"Finally, I heard a voice saying, 'Ahoy there, in the yawl.' I looks around and there was this small schooner, maybe 60 feet or so, coming right at me out of the fog. I wave back to show them I was still alive and the schooner heaves up right next to me, a fine piece of sailing it was. A couple of strong arms grab me and hoist me aboard like I didn' weigh nuthin' at all. I almost floated up to the deck.

"I can use another drink ya know. Got to keep my whistle wet.

"Well on the schooner I got hustled off to the foc'sle and bedded down to warm up. Sweetest smelling hole I'd ever been in, too! I was awful cold! The cook came down with a big pot of hot coffee and the captain even poured a slug of whiskey into it. That did more to warm me up than anything else. I fell into a dead sleep. The next day I felt pretty good. My wet clothes had dried out and I went up on deck. Everyone aboard was happy to see me and asked a hundred questions about the wreck, what ship it was, where we was bound to, all that kind of stuff. One old feller even wanted to know who the president was? I thought that was pretty strange and all. After a bit the cook came up with a bowl of hot duff for me. Boy, I was treated well. The captain, whose name was Brown, if I remember right, tells me he is headed for Eagle Harbor on the Keweenaw with a cargo of mining machinery. There were a lot of crates on deck so I figured that's what was in there. But I don't remember any mining up there since the early days. Now it's all down toward Calumet and Red Jacket way. Well I calculated it ain't my business where he's going with what. Some of the passengers said they was miners and they were a rough looking lot, worse than the ones I would see in Marquette down from the iron mines out on the range. A couple of the other guys said they was lumbermen from Vermont, of all places. Even had a few so'jer boys on board, too. It was a real odd collection, but again, none of my affair. I get to jawin' with the mate and he tells me the little schooner is the *Merchant* out of the Soo. Now, being an old sailor man, I get to lookin' the ship over and notice she's top's'l rigged. Everything today is fore and aft, even those Canuck boats out of Kingston. It was a real odd boat.

"Well, I figure again, what the hell, I'll get off wherever she stops and count myself very lucky. And I was too, 'cause it turned out no other poor bastard got off the *Comrade*. They ended up on the bottom with her.

"It was really strange, we sail and sail and never get anywhere. The wind was always fair, a good northeast breeze and the schooner showing her heels. Must have been making eight knots, but we jess don't get nowhere. For three days we sailed like that. Hell, we should have made Fort William four times over!

"The grub's real good, duff and apple pie, good salt junk. The weather's fine and I don't stand no watches or do no work, so it's a real sailor's heaven. I mean, what more can you want? But I'm thinking something's wrong. I gets to ruminat'n' about it. Then I remembers about the *Merchant*. When I started sailin' I had a mate on the old *Lilly May* that had a habit of yarn'n' pretty good during the dog watches. One night he related the story of the old *Merchant* and her strange fate. If'n I recollect right, she left the Soo in 1847, that's before they even built the big ditch, bound up for the Keweenaw with mining supplies. She never made it, jess dropped through a crack in the lake. Never found a trace of ship or men!

"I finally figger out I'm on a damned ghost ship! We ain't ever going to get to Eagle Harbor or any place else for that matter. Jess spend the rest of eternity sailing to nowhere. Now, I don't know if I am dead or alive or what. And there was nuthin' ghostly about the schooner either, solid decks and people that talked with you just like I am. Hell's bells, I gettin' fed three good squares a day, got no watch to pull and always a fair wind! Maybe's I'm in heaven!

"Anyways, I resolved to get off the ship. I waited until dark, then hauled up my yawl that she'd been draggin', slipped the painter and rowed for all I was worth. I wanted to git as far away as I could before any of them knew I was gone. I rowed for about an hour when a blow came out of the northwest, had a good kick to it, too! It was all I could do to keep the bow into the waves. All the next day it blew pretty good, too. I was sure I was a goin' to loose that yawl, but she kept me up real good. About dusk, I saw the Michigan coast three or four miles in. There wasn't anything I was goin' to do to pick a land 'n' spot. A couple of hours after dark the yawl went over in the surf and I tumbled out into the water. The next wave knocked me flat, as did the next couple. Eventually I ended up on the beach half drowned. I huddled behind some rocks to stay out of the wind 'til morning broke, then

Is the ghost of the old schooner Merchant still sailing the lakes? C. PATRICK LABADIE

hiked inland. I came across some railroad tracks and waited. A couple of hours later, a lumber train came slowly down the tracks and I hopped on the last car. I rode for an hour or so, 'til we reached the edge of a town. I hopped off an' followed the tracks in. I didn't want no run-in with a rail dick. Pretty soon I recognized the place as Marquette. I had shipped plenty of times out of there.

"I slid on down to Lake Street and into Raymond's Bar and who should I see but old Captain Pete. I'd shipped with him on the *Exile* the season before and she was anchored out in the bay. I explain'd I needed a berth, that I had a run-in with a mate on another vessel and jumped ship. I don't think he believed me, but he still stood me to a drink and signed me up. Next morning, I'm aboard the schooner bound for Cleveland. I didn't say nuttin' 'bout the *Comrade* or the ghost *Merchant*.

"I ain't never told nobody about what happened to me. They wrote the whole crew of the *Comrade* off, that every one of them drowned when she foundered. Never even found a single floater.

"I didn't want to disillusion 'em none, 'cause I was hitched to a gal named Sadie. Really got plastered one night in One-Eyed Mike's in Bay City and she latched on to me something awful. Took me upstairs to one of the little rooms in the catacombs and jess turned me inside out! Next morning was a Sunday, so she drug me across Water Street to one of the gospel preachers and before I knowed it I was married to her! Well, for a while it was okay, maybe even better than that. I set her up in one of the cheap boardin' places a block back and it was our little nest. Regular good husband I was, too, even for a sailor. Brought my pay home after every trip and didn't even visit the gals in the ore towns. Hell, Sadie could teach them tricks anyhow.

"Anyways, I got home after a trip, walked into the rooms and there she was with another sailor. Caught 'em both right in the act. Well, I grabbed the guy and put him right through the window. We was on the second floor so he landed with a helluva crash. Walked away, though, limping bad like, but moving under his own power. Come to think of it, him going down the street in his red woolies was kind'a funny. I smashed Sadie good, too, knocked a couple of teeth out I'm sure. Her playing around on me just wasn't right, no how.

"I walked out of there and never looked back. The *Exile* wasn't goin' to leave for a couple more days, so I shipped on the *Comrade,* 'cause she was goin' out quick. Figured the law would be looking for me, with a complaint from either Sadie or the boyfriend. Ain't been back to Bay City since. With the *Comrade* gone with all hands, I'm in the clear. Far as any of 'em know, I'm drowned.

"Well, I ain't got long left. That doc 'round the corner says a couple of months, maybe. I wanted somebody to know about what really happened on Lake Superior that trip, both to the *Comrade* and on that damned ghost schooner too. So laddie, if'n you're goin' ta follow them lakes, stay clear of boats like that barge I was on, an keep yer eyes sharp for the ghost ships, too!"

Lester River Revisited

When I wrote the "Lester River Phantom" segment for *Haunted Lakes,* I thought I was recording an isolated incident, a one-of-a-kind event. I was wrong! Soon after the book was published I received a letter from another witness to a very similar event in the same area.

The second incident occurred in July 1998. The weather was perfect, bright sun and no fog. Visibility was excellent. The observer was driving north on Highway 61 between Duluth and

60

Two Harbors, Minnesota, enjoying the magnificent vistas of the forest and lake. As the road twisted, she looked out over the water and saw a boat very close to shore, far closer than any other vessel she had seen. It wasn't as big as the ones she watched go under the lift bridge in Duluth and seemed to be very old. It was completely black and there was no discernable name or number. Taken with the strange ship, she quickly pulled off the road and looked back to look the boat over closer. There was nothing there. The boat was gone!

Later, when she read *Haunted Lakes* and the story of the "Lester River Phantom," she realized what she had seen. In every way, with the exception of the black smoke, the sighting was identical with that of the "river phantom."[12]

The Boat's Gone!

The following piece was written by a popular Great Lakes writer. It is reproduced with the stipulation that his name not be used.

"I got a good one of my own to tell, as long as you don't let it blow my reputation as a researcher and such…. T'was in August of 1983, and my folks and I were camped in the motor home at the Soo. The campgrounds just above Mission Point to be exact. It was pre-dawn, and like a good little boat-nut I got up long before the sun so I could shower and dress and be ready to take photos at first light.

"It was a clear night as I went into the shower facility, but when I came out about 20 minutes later, one of those famed Soo fogs was really setting in, and the visibility was dropping fast. From the shower room I saw two amber masthead lights going down river. I kept a close eye on them as they headed down the river and as I walked back to the motor home. They were just too close together to be a big laker, I guessed about the size of a 200- to 300-footer, perhaps a saltie, I figured. The fog was setting in so fast that the whole thing was gone by the time I got into the motor home and turned on the scanner. That was just in time to hear Soo Control closing the river. I figured that was good because the odd boat that I saw would be just around Mission Point and would have stopped there – when the fog lifted, I could just walk down and see who it was.

"I spent the morning telling my brother about the strange boat and guessing who it may be. We speculated for hours about which boat it may be and I told him that as soon as the fog lifted all bets would be settled because she'd be right in front of us. The fog held until just before noon, then lifted rapidly. I walked down to the point and looked, but nothing was there! The *Bevercliffe Hall* was just above the rock pile downbound, and the *Herbert C. Jackson* was just below the point, upbound and the *Mesabi Miner* was downbound with another 'footer' ahead of her, but nothing else. No salties, no tugs, nothing! I kept on the scanner all the rest of the day, but there was nothing smaller than the *Jackson* in that river all day…. Spooky, eh? I'll never forget those amber colored lamps on those two high masts, and I've been scratching my head about that one for many years since."

CHAPTER 3

Shore Ghosts

A Campfire Story

"My grandfather always used to tell this story when we visited his camp. The camp was up near Bayfield, Ontario, on the south end of Lake Huron. We just called it 'camp,' but over the years it grew fairly large. The main house was a regular-sized home and there was a big barn, boathouse and some smaller buildings dating from when the family first got the property back in the late 1800s. Every summer my brother and I, as well as half a dozen cousins, went up there for a couple of weeks in July. It was always a lot of fun, swimming, fishing and just fooling around in the woods. Grandfather had a sauna right down by the lake and we would fire it up as hot as we could, bake for a while, then run and jump in the lake.

"The last night we were there he always had a big bonfire down on the beach and we cooked hot dogs and marshmallows. Grandfather used the occasion to tell some great ghost stories after we finished eating.

"Our favorite was the one we called, 'the dripping ghosts.' It wasn't all that much of a story, but we liked it. Maybe it was because it supposedly happened right on the beach where we had the fire. The atmosphere was right, too, the dying embers of driftwood, flickering shadows from the trees and people moving, the dark and whispering lake – it was all very spooky.

"Anyway, as grandfather told it, way back in the 1890s, when his father fished and cut wood in the area, there was a big storm on the lake. The ship *Nassau* was caught out in it and after a terrible

63

battle with the waves, sank off Bayfield. The whole crew perished in the storm. Some tried to escape in the lifeboat, but they were lost, too. Many of their bodies were found washed up on the beach we were standing on. The story goes that a year to the day after the wreck, his father was walking along the shore at night when he heard yells and screams coming from the lake. It was too dark for him to see anything, but he could hear the cries for help. A few minutes later he saw a lifeboat heading for shore. In a little bit it slid right up on the beach.

"Half a dozen rough looking guys climbed out of the boat. Great grandfather ran up to them and asked what happened, but got no answer, just cold stares from lifeless eyes.

"Great-grandfather had a cabin in the woods, just up from the beach. In fact it's still there. It's the building we all used to stay in, kind of a bunkhouse today.

"These guys are soaking wet, drenched to the bone. Great-grandfather tells the men to follow him to his cabin to warm up and get some hot coffee. So the little band starts out with great-grandfather in the lead with an oil lantern to light the way and the men following silently behind. Every time he looked back they were all there, but answered none of his questions. Finally, he reached the cabin. When he turned around to tell them to go in, there was no one behind him! A few seconds before they were all there. Then they just went, 'poof.' Great-grandfather ran back along the trail to the lake and searched the beach but found nothing. Even the boat was gone.

"It was only after Great-grandfather thought about it that he realized the date and the earlier loss of the steamer *Nassau* exactly a year before. He figured that he had seen the ghosts of the crew trying to reach safety! The following year, Great-grandfather was going from the cabin down to the lake for water when he met the crew coming up again! They walked right past him like he wasn't there. The ghost crew went nearly up to the cabin door before vanishing before his eyes. He always said every year they would come back and do the same thing. Grandfather said his father once took him down to see the ghosts. As they watched from the side of the trail, the crew marched silently past then disappeared. When his mother found out about their adventure, she was really mad and made his father promise never to take him again."

Author's note: When I checked on this story I discovered there was no *Nassau* lost in Lake Huron, however there was a wooden lumber hooker *Nashua* wrecked on October 4, 1892, off Bayfield,

Ontario. She was downbound for Toledo when she foundered in a gale, taking all aboard down with her. Is it logical to assume that over the span of several generations, *Nashua* became corrupted into *Nassau* and became the basis for this story?[13]

The Squeaky Bed

"When I was a kid my grandfather owned an old-time grocery store just up from the Cleveland waterfront. It was one of those places where he butchered in the back and cut the meat to order. A big wood-paneled cold room stood behind his meat counter. When he opened the door you could see whole sides of beef hanging by massive silver hooks, as well as string after string of sausage links. In the front of the store, he had all the regular canned and boxed goods, as well as barreled vegetables. Both he and Grandmother ran the store and I remember they did a good business with the boats.

"He had an old Ford truck and sometimes I helped him deliver orders down to the docks. Grandfather liked the boats because they always paid their bills on time – something that was often a problem with other customers. The second floor of the building was empty. Grandfather never wanted anyone to go up there, *ever!* Instead of living upstairs, as was common for these small businesses, they lived in an apartment next door.

"When I got older, I worked in the store after school stocking shelves, putting orders together and delivering them and cleaning up. Both grandparents were getting on in years and they really appreciated my effort.

"There was something strange however. Sometimes in the late afternoon, I would hear sounds from upstairs. Nothing scary, maybe steps like someone walking around or doors opening and shutting. The weirdest of all was the sound of bedsprings, just like someone was jumping on a bed! Several times, I thought I heard voices. A couple of times, I asked my grandparents what it was, but they always said something about it being the wind or perhaps mice.

"I always was an adventurous kid, so I resolved to try to find out what was making the noise. One day I had my chance. A friend of my grandparents died and they went to the funeral. Since it was summer and I was off from school, I said I would mind the store while they were gone.

"It was one of those gloomy rainy days that are made for this kind of spooky exploring. I was a little apprehensive about it but decided that this was my big chance, so I had to take it. I knew where the key was kept hanging on a hook next to the cooler, took it and opened the big padlock. The door was very stiff, the hinges really squealing as I pulled it open. It was evident that the door had not been opened in a very long time. There was a long narrow stairway leading up. I had an old flashlight with a weak yellow beam and using it to guide me, I carefully climbed to the upper landing.

"There was a long dark hallway running the length of the building with doors off to each side. The only light came from a window at the far end. It reminded me of an old hotel. Carefully I opened the door nearest to me and looked in. It was very small with an old bed on one side, a chest of drawers on the other and a bare wooden chair. A dirty window was on the wall opposite the door. Otherwise the room was empty.

"As I walked down the hall, I noticed that each room was numbered with a little enamel tag. I checked half a dozen on the way and each was about the same, containing a bed, chest and chair. The dust lay heavy everywhere. No one had been up here for a very long time.

"Just before I reached the end of the hall I heard a door open behind me. I turned quickly and thought I saw the outside door just shutting. Then there was the unmistakable sound of footsteps coming toward me in the hall. They stopped abruptly about halfway down and a door on the left opened, then shut. I stood where I was and shook for a couple of minutes, then got ahold of myself and went down the hall to the room.

"I stopped at the door, took a deep breath and slowly opened the door. The room had the standard bed, chest and chair as well as several other items. A clothes tree in the corner had a moth-eaten woman's dress hanging from it, and a china wash basin and pitcher set was on the chest. Next to it was a whisky bottle and two glasses. A small rug covered the middle of the floor. A set of woman's high button shoes were in the corner. A pair of men's dark trousers lay over the back of the chair and a black coat hung from one of the spindles. A set of men's boots was in front of the chair. Everything was heavily covered in dust.

"I saw no one in the room, but as I stood in the doorway the mattress began to move! Slowly at first, then faster and faster in a rhythmic up and down motion. The noise was exactly what I had heard downstairs. The center was depressed too, just as if someone were laying in it. I also heard heavy breathing and it wasn't my own. After several minutes the sound and motion stopped. Again everything was silent and motionless. I decided it was time to get out fast! I had just started down the stairs when I clearly heard a woman's voice ask, 'Same time next week, Frank?' A man's voice replied, 'Yea, Gracie, I'll be back.'

"I ran down the stairs, slammed the door and put the padlock back on it. I never said anything about what I had seen. After my grandparents died, the property was sold to another grocer. He tried to rent out the rooms upstairs to boarders but couldn't make a go of it. No one would stay there very long. I understand that he lost the building in a foreclosure to the bank. Today the building is long gone and the land is a parking lot, I think.

"I always wondered just what I had seen that day and heard all the other times. I knew it was some kind of ghostly experience, but whose ghost? I later found out that the building had been an old-time sailors' bar, a bucket-of-blood type of place for sailors on a run ashore. The drinking, dancing and fighting was all done downstairs while the ladies were upstairs. From what I read, the girls would either pick up the men in the bar or the men would arrange for a particular girl with the madam. Eventually, under the pressure from the reform movement, the police closed down all the sporting houses, at least in that part of town. Because of the reputation of the place, Grandfather got it for a very cheap price. He must have known something about the ghosts upstairs since, to my knowledge, he never tried to do anything with it, just sealed it up and forgot about it.

"The more I think of it though, the more I laugh. When we think of a ghost story, it's always something scary – moans, groans, rattling chains, that kind of thing, maybe even a vengeful spirit coming back to haunt the living. Probably that's all Hollywood anyway. When I reflect on it, what I saw was really the opposite. They may have scared the wits out of me, but really it was just a couple of spirits still getting it on. It's nice to know you can still do that in the spirit world."[14]

The Sailor Ghost of Sodus Point

Sometimes ghostly activities even make it into the local newspaper. A case in point is that of the sailor ghost of Sodus Point on Lake Ontario. The following is taken from the *Rochester Democrat & Chronicle* of Rochester, New York.

"Sodus, May 12, 1921 – That ghosts have a decided notion that the resting places of their corporeal remains should abide in peace without disturbance, even to the point of due reverence for the markers of their graves, has been demonstrated to at least one man in this town. Such a demonstration has come home to George Carson, of Sodus, caretaker of Point Charles, on Sodus Bay, for the cottage association, where during the summer season the elite of the resort are found in large numbers. It appears that Carson's troubles, as he relates them, came through the thoughtless removal of a marker indicating the spot where a drowned sailor was buried in 1857. This he did while engaged in his work of renovating the lawns and getting things fixed up for the opening of the summer homes. To make the story understandable, it is necessary to relate the history of the grave, on the edge of the bank about 20 feet south of where one of the largest cottages now stands.

"In the spring of 1857 there was found by Henry Rogers, on the bar connecting Point Charles with the mainland, the body of a dead sailor. He was a French-Canadian and had his name tattooed on his arm. The body was buried in its present grave, and for many years whispered assertions were made that peculiar mournful sounds could at times be heard in the vicinity of the grave during hard northeastern storms. Only once before the recent experience of Mr. Carson did any alleged apparition appear and that was in the year 1917, and it was kept a sort of circle secret until the second recent manifestation.

"It was in the summer of 1917, late in August, that in one of the cottages a party of three sat at the table in the dining room having a midnight lunch: the cottage owner, his sister and a man from New York. At the time there was a bad northeastern storm and as the clock struck 12 they heard knockings on the wall. There would be several rappings and then they would stop for a brief interval, so the story goes. This was kept up for nearly 10 minutes and it was thought that someone was playing a trick. After awhile the men decided to investigate and leaving by a rear door they took different directions, to meet on the front veranda. As they met one of them saw sitting on a bench between the cottage and the shore a white form. They called the sister to come out and the three claimed they watched the white figure rise from the bench, walk over to the grave and raise both hands above his head and disappear in the grave. The next day the men placed a marker on the head of the grave reading: 'To the Memory of the Dead Sailor Buried Here in 1857.'

"The incident did not get out of the circle until recently, when Mr. Carson had his experience. In cleaning up the lawn he toppled over the marker and with the rubbish the marker disappeared. That same night, he says, the realization came home to him that the marker could not that easily be disposed of. From his quarters on the point, he strolled out about 9 o'clock that evening, thinking to add the benefits of a constitutional to the enjoyment of a cigar. When nearing the old grave on the lawn he was 'scared stiff' by a full-length view of the old sailor ghost, pacing between the bench and the grave. Mr. Carson says he is not easily alarmed and he held his ground. He shouted a lusty 'Hey there' and the apparition proceeded to the grave, he relates, where with uplifted form it disappeared from view into the grave. The next day the first piece of business on the docket for Mr. Carson was the recovery of the old grave marker from the rubbish heap. Restoration was at once attended to and now all is serene again on Point Charles."15

Pultneyville, Lake Ontario's Ghostly Village

About 18 miles west of Rochester, New York, right on the shores of Lake Ontario, is the small, quiet village of Pultneyville. It is named for Sir William Pultney, an English baronet. Over its long existence it was home to many people and enterprises. Today some folk believe that it is also home to a number of ghosts!

Pultneyville has a long and colorful history. The area was first used by the French in 1678 when they traded with the local Native Americans. Situated at the mouth of Salmon Creek, it was a natural location for commerce to blossom. While the lake and creek were the major transportation routes, a foot trail also ran through the region. Unfortunately the local swamp was a breeding ground for "fevers," a disease that killed many early settlers.

Permanent settlers began to arrive in 1806, attracted by the moderate Lake Ontario climate and stands of good hardwood trees. Some of the early arrivals were displaced New Englanders used to nautical life. It is likely that they looked at the broad expanse of the lake with a degree of longing for home. Soon agriculture took hold and with true Yankee efficiency farms were producing more than they could consume and the surplus was being shipped by schooners and steamers. Fruit was a major part of the export produce. A small local shipping industry blossomed, as did a diminutive iron foundry. The local hardwood provided the wood for homes, ships and charcoal for the furnace. Grist mills, tanneries and lumber mills completed the economic activity.

Village life focussed on the lake. In the 1820s the government provided a breakwater to help protect the harbor, and a customs officer was stationed Pultneyville until 1892. When the railroad arrived in 1874 the majority of commercial shipping shifted to nearby Williamston. In the years before the Civil War, some of the homes in the village were used as stations for the underground railroad, helping to move fugitive slaves to freedom. One home was built with three special secret rooms just to hide the "passengers."

It is expected that a town as old as Pultneyville would have a couple of haunted houses, but it seems to have more than its fair share. The old Cragg house is one of those places considered to be haunted.

The home was built in 1870 by James Cragg, an English immigrant. Supposedly he obtained his money fraudulently by telling people in England that he was going to use it to establish missionaries to convert the Indians. Instead, he used the money to build his own home! On his death, the house passed to his daughter and eventually in 1929 to a Jennie Stell. She opened it as a boardinghouse. This was during the Depression and business was so bad that she was forced into a foreclosure sale. She was apparently very bitter about the sale and wrote a letter in 1939 to the buyers which was strangely threatening. In it she intimated that she would haunt the house on her death!

She seems to have kept her promise. The present owner, descendants of the family who bought the house from Stell, have had numerous experiences with what is thought to be her ghost. Many times overnight guests have come down from the third floor bedrooms and inquired if there were ghosts in the house. They complained of hearing unusual noises and being wakened in the middle of the night because the bed was moving! The bed in question was very heavy, so the force needed must have been considerable. The weird activity lasted only for a couple of nights, then everything calmed down. It was as if Mrs. Stell just grew used to their presence.

During recent renovations, Mrs. Stell was especially active, so much so that the painters called the house "spook central." In one incident, two painters were working on the first floor when one asked the other what color paint was needed in a particular room. The second said to check with the owner. He had heard her walking around upstairs all morning. Of course when the painter went up, no one was there. In another incident, three of the men had flat tires on the same day, one on the way to work and the other two in the driveway. Another painter fell off a ladder and refused to return to the house. A spray paint can exploded when another painter walked past it. It would seem that Jennie Stell didn't like the color scheme!

The owner says she feels the strongest sense of presence in the old nursery and on the third floor. On several occasions she has gone into the nursery in the middle of the night, found her child awake and sensed another presence in the room. At different times, she and her husband have awakened at night frightened, then been lulled off to sleep by a feeling of goodwill.

When her eldest child was 4 years old, he was afraid of anyone with white hair and wrinkles. What had happened to make him this way? Had he seen something in the house?

In one especially scary incident, the parents left the children with a baby sitter. When they got back home later that night, the sitter was in a fright. It seems she was busy in another room, listening for the baby on a monitor. She heard the child cry, followed immediately by a voice, "Oh, it's all right, it's all right." When the sitter rushed into the room, only the baby was there. Could the monitor have somehow intercepted another house, or was it …?

A farmhouse along the lake has also been the scene of mysterious happenings. Once the owner stopped home to make a telephone call and hearing something being dragged across the floor upstairs, surmised it was his wife moving an old trunk. He yelled up to her that he was leaving, but getting no response assumed she did not hear him and he left. Outside he met her returning from a friend's house. If she was outside, who was upstairs dragging the trunk across the floor? Together they searched the upstairs and found nothing – everything was in its proper place. On other occasions footsteps and knocking at the front door have been heard. No reason for the sounds is ever found.

In another home, a rug was the scene of an unexplained phenomenon. The distinct image of a man would appear on the rug but only after dark. Never during daylight. Cleaning the rug had no effect. Was it a bizarre trick of the light, or something else?

Perhaps the most famous haunted house in Pultneyville is that of Captain Horatio Throop. Born in nearby Williamson in 1807, he had a long career as a sailor, shipbuilder and businessman. He started as a boat builder at age 14 and soon was sailing as master of his own ships. He built his home in Pultneyville in 1832.

Today the house is a popular bed-and-breakfast inn, with its own permanent guest. Past owners say strange footsteps have been heard pacing back and forth in the empty upstairs hallway. The scraping sounds of furniture being dragged across the floor also echo eerily on the second floor. When checked, nothing has been moved and everything remains in its proper place. Family members report feeling a kind of force or energy in the house. This feeling is especially strong in the basement, back hall and in a small bedroom upstairs.

One overnight guest in the bedroom knew nothing of the house's history when he snuggled down in the comfortable bed looking forward to a good night's sleep. The next morning he related a most extraordinary dream. He saw a "man in old fashioned clothes doing something with windmills." The family knew old captain Throop had been an inventor who experimented with wind devices.

The family attempted to turn the small bedroom into a music room but the spirit defeated them. They moved a strong table stand to the room and placed a stereo on it. The stand collapsed suddenly, sending the stereo crashing to the floor. It would not be a music room!

In another instance the iron statue of Throop's dog, "Jeba," flew off the window sill to the floor, breaking an ear off. The statue is very heavy and such an accident is inconceivable.

One of the truly unique things about the house is the existence of two "witch bottles" in the ceiling. The bottles are made of green blown glass and set into the ceiling top down. Still tightly corked, it looks like each has the body of a spider and remains of a web inside. In some instances, pieces of mirrors and small shards of glass with salt and vinegar were sealed inside such bottles. The bottles are then blessed and sealed in the house. The salt and vinegar represent cleaning, the mirror is to reflect negative energy to the sender and the glass shards to trap evil energy. The bottles were found when the house was being remodeled. Why they were placed there and their purpose is unknown, but it is surmised that they were to ward off evil spirits.

It is believed that the ghost that walks the old house is that of the captain's nephew Horatio Throop Wilcox. "Rashe," as he was known to the family, lived for a time in the house. He seems to have been a bright young lad with an ambition to go to sea that his uncle would not support. Rashe kept a journal during the period 1859-60 when he was 18 years old. This document gives the impression that he was also very unhappy and perhaps emotionally disturbed. During this period he recorded attending the services of many different religious denominations, but seems to have been most taken with spiritualism. He was ill for some time, but no one took it seriously. They should have. He died in his small upstairs bedroom on November 26, 1862, at the age of 21.

At least one family was forced to leave the house by the overwhelming sense of presence. It was so unsettling they felt they had no choice but to flee.

Why is Pultneyville such a friendly home to those from another world? Perhaps it's the sense of community, of quiet, a place where the pace of change is just a little slower.[16]

Bay Cliff's Restless Spirit

About 25 miles northwest up the Lake Superior coast from Marquette, Michigan, is the small village of Big Bay. An old lumber town, at one time its mills made bowling pins and wood panels for the old Ford "woodies." Today Big Bay is a fine little community focusing on enjoying the better things in life: hunting, fishing, snowmobiling and hiking as the seasons allow.

Two prominent local institutions are the beautiful Big Bay Lighthouse bed-and-breakfast inn and Bay Cliff Health Camp. The lighthouse story, including its many ghosts, is told in the original *Haunted Lakes* book. The Bay Cliff story follows.

Bay Cliff Health Camp is a non-profit, summer therapy camp for children who require occupational, speech, vision or hearing therapy. Founded in 1934 as a care center for undernourished and underprivileged children, over the years its focus shifted to the present therapy emphasis. The camp site proper is a former dairy farm.

There are stories that the camp is haunted, but by whom or what is not known. The 134-acre camp is deep in the north woods, with one side bordering tall sandstone cliffs overlooking Lake Superior. Surrounded by woods on the other three sides, it is an isolated location. At night, with the wind whistling through the trees and low clouds scudding before the full moon, it can be a very creepy place, especially to people not used to life deep in the north woods.

However, the camp is not always used by handicapped children. In some instances children from local schools have the opportunity to spend time there enjoying the wonders of nature.

This story comes from a former counselor and it is based on her experiences at the camp. There is an L-shaped building containing three large and several smaller rooms. Known as "Sam's Place," it is named for a child who supposedly died there. Often this building will house the most difficult medical cases. Some believe that the building, especially the center room, is haunted by Sam's spirit. The room contains several pieces of old furniture, a piano and numerous plaques on the walls. Some counselors have refused to stay in the room or building. In the recent past the building has been unused, except for storage.

One tale goes that two counselors were asleep in each of the two end rooms. At 4 a.m., one counselor was awakened by a bright light in the center room. The counselor checked her girls and finding everything fine, went back to bed, thinking another counselor must have turned on the light. The next morning, she asked the other counselor about the light and was told that she had also been awakened by it, checked her charges and went back to sleep, believing it was turned on by the other counselor. Once they got over their mutual shock and confusion, neither would go in the center room again.

The next year, two groups of girls and their counselors were staying in the Sam's Place cabin. Late one night, they all were badly scared when a heavy plaque in the center room fell from the wall in the middle of the night waking everyone. It took a while, but finally the counselors were able to settle the children down for the rest of the night. When they came back from breakfast the next morning, they all had another shock. The plaque was back in its holder, but upside down! Since all of the girls, counselors and staff were at breakfast together, there was no opportunity for "skullduggery." But then who, or what, had replaced the plaque?

There was another incident at Sam's Place. One Wednesday night after a dance, the occupants of Cabin 11 heard a thunderous noise in the room. Looking around, they saw some lights shining in the screened-in room and thought it was some counselors with flashlights. Running outside to look, they were startled to find no one there. Where were the lights coming from? Two counselors at the auditorium also heard the noise and came running to the cabin. Entering it, they found a silver plaque face up on the table. Evidently it had fallen off the wall and made the loud noise. Engraved on the plaque was:
"In Memory of
Francis McKerchie
November 12, 1965-July 14, 1980
At this spot he met his friends,
They shared their secrets
They laughed …
He left here happy."

There was another weird incident in May 1996. It was a long tradition that the last night of camp the counselors would stay-up all night in the auditorium. It was just a night of good fun, singing, listening to music, eating, telling stories and finally watching the sun come up over Lake Superior. About 2 a.m., several counselors decided to take a walk to the old gazebo. Since the staff didn't want campers to play on it, the area around it was marked off with yellow tape. The cabin known as Sam's Place was several hundred feet beyond it. The night was absolutely still without a whisper of wind.

As the counselors approached the tape, it began to move rapidly, giving the impression that unseen hands were shaking it. One of the counselors went up to the tape and said "Stop" in a loud, commanding voice. The tape went still! A few minutes later it started up again and the counselor ordered it to stop. Again it stopped! Shaken by the bizarre experience, the counselors ran back to the auditorium. None left again until dawn!

The next morning the counselors noticed that the door to Sam's Place was wide open. The evening before it was securely latched. What had opened it? Did something come from the room to the nearby gazebo? Was the ghost from Sam's Place the "tape shaker."

Big Bay certainly has its share of ghosts. Besides the ones at the lighthouse and health camp, it is also said that the Thunder Bay Inn might have a spirit or two. These are only the ones we have heard stories about. What other tales lurk in the dark shadows of this small Lake Superior community?[17]

Minnie Quay

About five miles north of Port Sanilac, on Michigan's thumb, is the small town of Forester and another ghost, Minnie Quay. Forester used to be a busy lumber town, but when the trees went, so did the people. Today it's primarily composed of summer cabins.

The story goes that Minnie was a young girl of nearly 15 that fell in love with a sailor. As a busy lumber port, Forester had a long pier out into Lake Huron and likely Minnie met her sailor right off the ship.

In any case, he was later lost in a storm in the spring of 1876. Despondent over his death, Minnie was said to have waved goodbye to some loafers in front of a local store, then calmly walked off the end of the pier and drowned herself.

Apparently, even in death she not did find her sailor man, for today it is claimed that her ghost walks the lakeshore, still searching for her long-lost love. It is even said that she has been sighted in the water, trying to lure other young girls to an early death![18]

Drowning Man

There are some ghosts that bridge the gap between land and water. The crawling ghost of Calvary Cemetery is one of them. The cemetery is located right on the border between Chicago and Evanston, Illinois. Established in 1859, it is one of the oldest in the area and looks out on Sheridan Road toward Lake Michigan.

There are persistent reports of the ghost of a drowning man sighted in the lake just opposite from the cemetery. After the figure sinks for the final time, he is seen to crawl up the shore, cross the road and disappear in the cemetery.[19]

Some sources identify the ghost as a Navy pilot killed in an attempt to land on one of the small training aircraft carriers used on the lake. During World War II, thousands of naval aviators trained on Lake Michigan. A number were killed in accidents.

A Saginaw Ghost Story

During the heyday of logging and sailing, Saginaw, Michigan, was one of those towns where lumberjacks and sailors both mixed and "mixed it up." The city had its fair share of spirits, most bottled, but some were more vaporous. The following is an example of what happens when the dead collide with the living.

"A GHOST STORY
"How a Saginaw Family Was Visited by 'That Strange Man' – A Mysterious Affair – A Gun Fired and A Wounded Man Groaned – He Could Not Be Found

"For several months past, a family living on what is known as 'Big Ditch' on Mason Street in Saginaw City have been troubled with what they supposed to be home breakers or meddlesome persons. Accordingly, a few weeks since, the head of the family loaded his shotgun pretty heavily and one night stationed himself a short distance from his house in the corner of his yard, and awaited his usual visitors. At about midnight he noticed a man, or what he supposed to be his living tormenter, prowling around the door and, taking accurate aim, fired, and, as he supposed, slightly wounding him.

"Immediately upon the discharge of the gun, the man groaned somewhat and, on running to the spot to clutch his intruder, the shootist, to his great surprise, saw him vanish. It now seems that the family, as the neighborhood gossip says, has been troubled for several months past almost beyond endurance, and more especially during the past two weeks. In the evening when any of the family are reading, there will be mysterious figures pass between the reader's eyes and the book, and the light will go out and the fire in the stove will really smother and go out. And not only are they troubled this way in the house, but when any of the family go out in the evening they are preceded through the yard by a ghostly pedestrian. In addition, to these manouverings [sic], the family at midnight are aroused and worried by mysterious rappings and rumbling noises. The inmates of the house, and also the neighbors, positively assert the house is haunted, as the visits of this strange man are altogether too numerous. We understand a party of gentlemen, by invitation of the owner of the house, intend spending a night there, when we expect to hear more in regard to these strange doings."[20]

Fort Ontario's Wandering Spirit

Although strictly not a nautical ghost story, the area in question is so completely wrapped into the maritime history of the Great Lakes as to make such minor distinctions irrelevant. The fort mentioned in this April 18, 1877, *Oswego Palladium* article is Fort Ontario.

"Oswego has never been noted for ghosts. In fact, there has hitherto been no trustworthy record of any Oswego ghost of any kind. Suddenly, without any previous announcement, and without the aid of any medium, an Oswego ghost makes his appearance, and in a short time wins the deserved reputation of being the most complete and successful ghost in this country or in Europe. Grain has lost its charm for the Oswego people and canals seem little better than muddy mockeries. Henceforth Oswego will be known as the great ghost center of the continent, and its inhabitants will take even a greater pride in their ghosts than the inhabitants of Chicago take in their pigs.

"On the evening of the 3rd of July last, a leading citizen of Oswego took his daughter to see the fireworks. Of course, that young lady remarked, 'O!' and also 'Gracious!' whenever a firework was produced; but equally, of course, she paid far more attention to contiguous young men than she did to the pyrotechnic display. On her way home she said, with a careless air, 'Pa,' – and whether she pronounced it 'pay' or 'paw' we are not informed – 'who was that young soldier who stood next to you?'

"The author of existence replied that he had not seen any destructive young man and was in the act of muttering a subdued anathema upon all young men when his daughter violently pinched his arm, and said in a sharp whisper – 'There he is now.'

"The leading citizen turned his head and saw a strange uniform, hastening apparently where glory, or at all events gin awaited him. The father explained that the young man was some strange kind of idiot who had picked up an old British uniform, and, with a view to contingencies, he warned his daughter that the man was, undoubtedly, a Canadian tramp, thirsting for spoons.

"The two went on their homeward way; the father subsequently went to bed and the daughter executed that mysterious feminine feat known as 'retiring.'

"On the next Friday evening, this same father was sitting with this same daughter in the dining room, when the sound of the piano in the parlor was heard. They both imagined that a book agent had surreptitiously gained admission to the house, and seizing the poker and the hot-water kettle, determined to reason mildly with the intruder. This latter, however, proved to be the same young man whom the daughter had gazed at under the pretense of fireworks. He arose, and bowing politely, introduced himself as George Fikes, formerly a private in the British army, who had died in Oswego, while in garrison, in the year 1782.

"Mr. Fikes made himself so pleasant that when, after a brief call, he prepared to vanish, he was asked to call again, which he regularly did every subsequent Friday evening. This leading citizen and his daughter for some time kept the fact that they had a ghostly visitor a profound secret, and only a fortnight since the father confided it to the editor of a local paper. That editor was permitted, under a solemn pledge of secrecy, to send a reporter to 'interview' Mr. Fikes, and that reporter has already had two long and absolutely worthless conversations with the ghost.

"According to this incompetent reporter, Mr. Fikes does not enter the door or even the window, but suddenly appears in the parlor of the leading citizen at the same hour on every Friday evening. He always wears the same old-fashioned British uniform of George III's reign, with the exception of his hat, which he is in the habit of frequently changing. When his interview is ended, Mr. Fikes vanishes as suddenly and unexpectedly as he appears. He does not go out of the door or sink into the floor, but he just vanishes in the most approved ghostly way. He is a polite, affable and accomplished gentleman, as the British private notoriously is, and the daughter of the leading citizen calls him 'Gweawge' and is evidently warmly attached to him. Careful search in the neighborhood of the old Oswego fort has been rewarded by the discovery of a tombstone bearing the name of 'George Fikes,' and the reporter has not the slightest doubt that the ghost is that of the identical George Fikes who died nearly a century ago. A ghost that can materialize itself without any medium and with a choice of hats; who will sit quietly in the parlor and converse with as much sweetness and light as though he were Matthew Arnold in a magazine article; who will play nicely upon the piano, and always vanish at an early hour, is clearly an immense improvement upon all previous ghosts.

"It must be said, however, that the reporter who has 'interviewed' Mr. Fikes on two successive Friday nights is a disgrace to his profession. Any real reporter with such opportunities would have had all the facts as to the other world out of Mr. Fikes in 15 minutes by the watch, but the Oswego reporter has drawn absolutely nothing from the ghost that was worth printing. He simply asked him a few questions as to his life in Oswego, as if any human being cared to know what a person condemned to live in Oswego in 1782 was accustomed to. He did not ask Mr. Fikes to describe the celestial world, and to explain the exact process of dying. He did not ask him if there are newspapers on the other side of the Styx, and if so, in what department of the spirit world they are published, and what is the average salary of a ghostly reporter.

"Mr. Talmadge recently informed drunkards that there is no 'rum' in hell – implying, of course, that there is abundance of that beverage in heaven; and yet this preposterous reporter never once asked Fikes if Talmadge had told the truth. All the questions that he did ask might just as well have been put to Mr. Bancroft or Mr. Parkman. They were mainly questions relating to the early history of Oswego, and were not only unimportant in themselves, but were valueless in relation to the ghost's identity. It is maddening to think that this ridiculous reporter has, together with the leading citizen and his daughter, a monopoly of Mr. Fikes, and that he is solemnly sworn not to betray the name of the leading citizen or to point out his house.

"This fine opportunity for obtaining the latest information as to the other world is thus thrown away. Perhaps in time the reporter, by mere accident, will ask an intelligent question; but unless he does, Mr. Fikes' return to earth will be of no benefit to anyone except the daughter of the leading citizen. Still the fact remains that Oswego has produced the champion ghost of this century, and only an ungenerous mind will refuse to give that city full credit for so able an achievement."[21]

The Crosswinds

Just down from the haunted White Lake Lighthouse, the story of which is told in the original *Haunted Lakes,* is the Crosswinds Restaurant, also said to have a resident spirit. White Lake came into being as a lumber town with sawmills dotting the Lake Michigan shore. The mills are all long gone and the buildings reused for other purposes. The Crosswinds, for example, is located in an old sawmill building.

The ghost in question is that of a young boy supposedly killed in some kind of an industrial accident while the building was still a sawmill. This was an age when young boys were expected to earn their keep and worked side-by-side with adult men. Deadly mishaps during this period of unguarded machinery and just plain dangerous working conditions were commonplace.

Restaurant workers claim to have seen the ghost of a small boy out of the corner of their eyes quickly flitting across the room. Patrons also have seen the apparition and asked the wait staff about the running boy. The ghost plays a number of pranks, the most common being pushing a shelf full of glasses to the floor. His antics were enough that the owners, apparently tired of replacing glassware, called in a clairvoyant and had a seance during which they asked him to stop breaking the glassware. Their effort was successful since the glassware no longer breaks although the ghost they named Oscar is still said to be speeding about the dining room.[22]

Johnsons Island Ghosts

If you are going to build a prison, Johnsons Island in Lake Erie is hard to beat as the perfect location. Approximately 300 acres in size, it is about two miles off the Ohio shore directly north of Sandusky. The Canadian shore is a long 30 miles to the north. During the Civil War, the island was indeed a prison, holding between 10,000 and 15,000 Confederate soldiers.

For the thin blooded Southerners, the cold blasts of a Great Lakes winter wind must have been hell itself. As a general rule, prisoners in any war are never given the best of quarters or rations and the men at Johnsons Island were no different. The icy wind cutting through their light clothing and whistling between the planks of their barracks walls took a terrible toll. Pneumonia and fevers carried away those weakened by the unaccustomed cold. While the camp's conditions never approached the horrors the South inflicted on the helpless Union inmates at Andersonville

Prison, for the men whose bones lay buried in the hated Yankee ground, such comparisons are of scant importance.

Virtually none of the confederate prisoners escaped. During the navigation season, the gunboat *Michigan* often anchored just offshore, training her guns on the prison walls to intimidate the inmates. In the winter, trekking 30 miles on Lake Erie's ice to Canada was virtually impossible. The prison compound consisted of 13 barracks buildings, all behind a 12-foot-high board fence. On the south side, the fence ran within a few yards of the bay. A gallery on the outside of the wall provided a walkway for the guards. During the summer, excursion steamers sometimes came right up to the camp so excursionists could jeer at the prisoners and taunt them with patriotic songs.

In retaliation for poor treatment of Northern men at Southern prisons, rations were often cut, which according to some accounts reduced the men to mere skin and bones, walking skeletons whose sunken eyes bore the sure mark of impending death. The estimated 200 men who did die were buried deep in good northern soil in the small cemetery on the northeast tip of the island. The original wooden grave headboards were replaced after the war with stones of Georgia marble, each that could be identified was engraved with the soldier's name, state and regiment. But 52 are carried as simply "unknown."

When the dreadful war ended, the prisoners were released and sent home, back to the land they fought so hard to save. The dead, however, stayed, forced to forever remain prisoners on Johnsons Island.

Some people believe that the island is haunted by the restless ghosts of the long dead rebels. Visitors have occasionally reported an overwhelming sense of dread while walking through the woods, as if someone they could not see were watching them. There have been other stories of hearing the faint strains of "Dixie" drifting softly on the gentle wind. Is it nothing, mere imagination or perhaps something more – the manifestation of a powerful yearning from men trapped forever in an alien land?[23]

The Tunnels

Keep your eyes sharp now! We're close to Kelleys Island and this is where it happens! I was downbound on a wind wagon in June of 1899. We were just a little behind the Olwill *when the damn miners pulled her down. Mind you, it was pretty sloppy that night, rough if you haven't been on the lake when she kicks up her heels. It was just about here it happened, too! I was at the wheel and having a helluva time holding her up. Old Sudsy was captain and he was an ornery cuss. Yell at me all night, but not lift a finger to help! The lazy bum! A couple of years later he got knifed in a saloon in Cleveland by one of the upstairs gals. He probably deserved it! Anyway, I'm working like the devil to keep her from going over, but I'm keeping one eye on the Olwill too, ya see. When she dropped into the trough she would disappear, then come up the other side. Well, she dropped and didn't come up! When she bottomed in the waves them damn miners just reached up and grabbed her and pulled her down! We sailed right past where she was and there wasn't anything left. Good boys on her, too! I used to drink with a few of them in Shady's. Damn shame it is!*

Kelleys Island is just a couple of miles out into Lake Erie from Marblehead, Ohio. The major natural resource on the island is limestone and it forms the basis for this story. Quarrying the limestone began in the 1840s. Although many men worked the quarry, it was the Italians who were the most skillful. Day after day and year after year, ship after ship carried the cut rock from the docks to points all over the lakes. It was good stone and in high demand.

As more and more rock was removed, the men gradually tunneled under Lake Erie. One day a terrible mistake was made. An overzealous foreman apparently ordered a crew to blast a shelf of rock that resulted in flooding the tunnel and drowning dozens of men. Supposedly most of the bodies were never recovered.

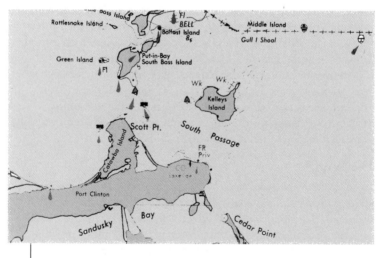

Some say the waters off Kelleys Island are filled with the spirits of lost sailors.

Soon after, ships began to sink in the area offshore of the island and sailors claimed to have heard the terrible wails of the drowned quarrymen echoing across the water at night. The sailors also said that the tunnel went under the lake so far that it nearly reached Marblehead! At night, the ghosts of the men marched up and down the tunnel, dragging heavy chains behind them. Their spirits sought vengeance on the sailors because the ships were owned by the greedy mine proprietors. When a ship passed overhead, it was said that the ghosts literally rose up from the deep to drag it down to the bottom. The October 17, 1936, loss of the *Sand Merchant* is often cited as the latest example of the quarrymen's revenge. Others include the schooner *Young America,* August 20, 1880, steamer *Margaret Olwill,* June 28, 1899, and steamer *Adventure,* October 7, 1903.[24]

Ghostly Sisters

The Great Lakes are filled with ghosts, or at least ghost stories. Sailors by their very nature are a superstitious lot, prone perhaps to seeing not only what is there, but also sometimes what *might* be there. Anyone who does not believe this simple fact has only to hike the sandy beach of Lake Superior's infamous shipwreck coast on a dark and stormy night or sail past Lake Michigan's Beaver Island when a blinding fog blankets out the known world. Under such circumstances, the imagination can be ratcheted up a notch or two and old stories of shipwreck and death, restless spirits or wandering ghosts assume a new credibility.

Although old lake sailors and the men of the U.S. Life-Saving Service knew the worst storms always come in November, they also were well aware that a "gagger" could blow up anytime. Such was the case on August 30, 1892.

A young surfman, Benjamin Truedell, was napping before his scheduled midnight beach patrol. Truedell was stationed at Lake Superior's Deer Park, the most westward of the four life-saving stations along Michigan's dreaded shipwreck coast. Mariners said that there was one wreck for every mile of the 40 mile stretch, and the bones of drowned sailors were buried in the beach to prove it! The other stations were at Vermilion Point, Crisp Point and the Big Two-Hearted River. Each was manned by a keeper or captain and six to eight surfmen. Their job was simple; to prevent shipwreck by warning vessels off the treacherous reefs and shore, or in the event of wreck, to rescue as many of the passengers and crew as possible.

The lifesavers had two principal methods of making a rescue. Either by using their 26-foot surfboat via a dangerous beach launch

Truedell later became the highly respected keeper of the Grand Marais, Michigan, Life-saving Station. T.R. RICHARDSON COLLECTION

through the breakers, or with a complicated breeches buoy apparatus. In the latter method, a light line was first shot over the wreck with a small cannon known as a Lyle gun. After the first line was used to haul successively heavier ropes, a breeches buoy was rigged between ship and shore and one by one the stranded victims were brought to safety.

Regulations required that each crew patrol the beach four miles left and right of the station every night. At the end point of each leg, the surfman either exchanged a brass token with a patrolman from the next station or, if he was from an end station, punched his time clock in at the key post. In fine summer weather beach patrol was an easy and pleasant walk. But during a screaming north gale, it was a miserable struggle against nature's fury. The night of August 30, 1892, was such a horrible night. Truedell was well-advised to try to rest before having to battle his way through the storm.

Truedell's sleep was anything but peaceful. As the fury of the wind tore at the wooden station house, rattling the windows, the surfman thrashed in his metal cot. Sweat beaded on his brow and his hands clenched into tight fists. He wasn't just dreaming, he was having a full-blown nightmare!

Interviewed many years later, he remembered the incident vividly. "At midnight when I was awakened to go on patrol, I leaped from my cot trembling and perspiring and glanced about wildly, for I had been dreaming of a wreck, a dream so realistic I still fancied myself on the beach. The delusion persisted in spite of (being among) my comrades, dressed in oilskins and carrying lanterns in the familiar surroundings of the station."

Noting Truedell's obvious distress, his crew mates asked what was the matter. He said, "I've had a most peculiar dream. A ship is going down somewhere. And a lot of people will go down with her."

His friends expressed disbelief, but Truedell only replied, "Mark my words. Tomorrow we will hear of a wreck!"

He went on to say, "I dreamed I was walking down the beach through the storm. I had not gone far before I became aware of another presence. It was a well-dressed man, obviously someone of position."

The strange specter moved out of the gloom and stepped directly in front of the lone surfman and started speaking. But in the roar of the breakers, Truedell could not make out the words. Three times the figure motioned out to the wild lake. As if in a last, desperate effort to make himself understood, the form moved so close to Truedell that his pleading face was right in that of the surfman's, then it just faded into the Stygian darkness.

When Truedell repeated the dream to the rest of the crew, they treated it as a joke. What else could it be? Truedell knew better. His mother was said to have had the gift of second sight and he did, too! Although he made his night patrol without incident he knew a wreck was in the offing.

The next day the lifesavers stopped chuckling about Truedell's dream. About noon, a man more dead than alive staggered into the warmth of the station messroom. Through chattering teeth he said he was Harry Steward, a wheelsman on the steamer *Western Reserve*. Bundled quickly into warm blankets from the wreck locker and given hot coffee, he collapsed on a bench for several long minutes. After a brief rest, he gathered his strength and mumbled out a tragic tale.

The big 301-foot, 2,392-ton *Western Reserve* was upbound light for Two Harbors, Minnesota. When she rounded Whitefish Point, a stiff gale was blowing from the northwest, but it was nothing the mighty steamer should be concerned with. Both Captain Albert Myers and Chief Engineer W.H. Seaman were veterans of the Great Lakes and accustomed to a bit of rough water.

The *Western Reserve* was a nearly new vessel, having been built only two years before by the Cleveland Shipbuilding Company. Already she had set several cargo records. On her last trip to Marquette, three weeks or so earlier, she loaded 2,608 tons of ore, more than a single vessel had ever carried out of the port before. Big things were expected of the *Western Reserve* and she was delivering them.

Along for the ride was her owner, Captain Peter G. Minch, his wife, Anna, their 10-year-old son, Charlie, and 7-year-old daughter, Florence. Accompanying them was his wife's sister, Mrs. Jacob Delker Englebry, and her 9-year-old daughter, Bertha. It was intended to be a fine end-of-summer vacation cruise. Until they rounded Whitefish Point, it had been a wonderful trip with calm waters and clear skies.

Despite the storm, all went well until about 9 p.m. when the steamer was 35 miles northwest of Deer Park. Without warning there was a violent jolt, followed by an equally ferocious shuddering. Forward motion ceased. The vessel had cracked clean across her spar deck just forward of the boiler house! She was rapidly heading for the bottom!

Quickly orders were passed to abandon her. All 21 crewmen and six passengers boarded two small yawls, one metallic and one wood. Captain Minch, his family and guests as well as some of the crew were in the wooden boat. Almost immediately on reaching the water the metal boat capsized. All of those aboard save one disappeared in the foaming seas. The lone survivor managed to

The big **Western Reserve** *foundered off the infamous shipwreck coast of Lake Superior.* MARINE HISTORICAL SOCIETY OF DETROIT

climb into the wooden boat. Minutes later, the 19 souls who were still alive watched in silent horror as the *Western Reserve* dove beneath the waves. From crack to sinking, a bare 10 minutes had passed!

In the prevailing sea conditions, all the survivors could do was to fight to keep the yawl's bow into the seas and bail for all they were worth. For 10 long hours they were blown before the furious wind and mountainous waves. About 7 a.m. on August 31, they had reached a point about a mile off the beach. There disaster struck again. A succession of steep breakers capsized the yawl spilling all aboard into the lake. Only wheelman Harry Steward made it to the safety of the shore. He claimed it took him two hours to struggle through the grasping seas.

Steward later stated, "I saw none of the occupants after starting for the shore, but the cries of the children, the screams of the women and moaning of the men were terrible for a few moments, then all was silent." After gathering his strength on the beach, he staggered off to the lifesaving station.

Immediately on hearing Steward's tale keeper John Frahm alerted the other stations and sent his crew to search the desolate beach in hopes of finding more survivors. No more were found. Steward alone had cheated the grim reaper.

However Truedell's nightmare wasn't finished. While sweeping the wave-washed beach, he discovered the body of a well-dressed man laying face down and partially buried in the sand. When he rolled him over and looked at his face he realized with a start that he was staring face-to-face at his nightmare. The specter who came to him in his dream was the same man who was laying cold dead on the beach gazing up at him with pleading eyes. From the engraved watch found in his pocket, he was identified as Captain Peter Minch. In Truedell's dream, Minch had desperately tried to warn of the wreck, but to no avail. Was he trying to make the lifesaver understand the importance of having men at the beach where the yawl capsized to rescue his family? Was it a dream communicating with the living?

As the days passed, other victims of the capsized boat also came ashore in the waves. Many were shipped to their homes for interment. Others, unclaimed by anyone, were laid to rest in the lonely dunes. Captain Frahm and his men always took the time to kneel and utter a short prayer over the unmarked grave of each of the unknown men.

It is said that on dark and stormy nights, when the surf runs high and the north wind howls like a goosed banshee, the hideous

The W.H. Gilcher *was the sistership of the ill-fated* Western Reserve. *K.E.*
THRO COLLECTION

shrill cries of the yawl's panic stricken occupants could still be
heard. Some even say the spirits of the drowned sailors crawl out
from their sandy graves to prowl the cold shore. For sometime
following the wreck, other sailors claimed that far out on the lake,
amid the billowing black waves, the ghostly form of the big steamer
was seen still plowing the upbound lane for Two Harbors, seeking
to finish her interrupted trip. The reports rarely made the
newspapers, even the marine columns didn't print such idle gossip.
But in the saloons where sailors met to hoist a drink or two, such
sightings were often compared. And it wasn't always the *Western
Reserve* that was seen. The ice-covered hull of the steamer
Bannockburn and tug *Lambton* also had their "see'ers." Some beery-
eyed mariners even said they could see the skeletal faces of crewmen
staring blankly out the pilothouse windows!

The *Western Reserve* had an identical sister, the *W.H. Gilcher,*
launched less than four months after the *Reserve.* They were as alike
as two vessels could be. All during the 1891-92 seasons, the pair
competed in a game of one-upmanship – one setting a cargo record
only to have it bested by the other.

Less than two months after the *Western Reserve* sank, the
Gilcher did too. On October 28, 1892, she was upbound for
Milwaukee with coal under Captain Leeds H. Weeks when she ran
into a strong gale in northern Lake Michigan. When the lake finally
calmed several days later, the steamer couldn't be found. She hadn't
made Milwaukee and wasn't sheltering behind some island or
ashore on a desolate beach. The steamer had simply "sailed into a
crack in the lake," as the old-time wind drivers said. Her crew of 18

must have finished the trip with her, because not a body was ever found. All that was eventually located was a small amount of debris on the shore of High Island, near Beaver Island. To the macabre, it was almost as though the *Gilcher* was still competing with her sister. One man escaped from the *Western Reserve,* but none got away from the *Gilcher!*

The experts, of course, examined the facts and offered several explanations for the loss of the *Gilcher:* that she struck a reef and quickly foundered, collided with the schooner *Ostrich,* also lost with all hands in the same storm, or suffered a brittle steel fracture, as they suspected the *Western Reserve* did. What these learned men couldn't explain were the claimed sightings of the steamer after she sank. Some old lake sailors believed that, like the *Western Reserve,* the *Gilcher* also reappeared on dark and stormy nights. Wraith-like, they claimed to have seen her steaming past Beaver Island, a dark phantom from the dead past. Were both ghostly sisters, spiritual rovers of the lakes, trying to finish one final trip, in competition to the last?

Neither the *Western Reserve* or *W.H. Gilcher* has been reported in recent years. Whether they finally made port or today's sailors are just too technologically astute to see what doesn't show on a radar screen is of course conjecture. But in the old days, when sail ruled the lakes, such ghost ships as the *Reserve* and *Gilcher* were very real. Maybe, somewhere far out on the open lake, when conditions are just right, they still are.

AFTERMATH

Truedell stayed in the Life-Saving Service, eventually rising to be keeper of the Grand Marais Station, 18 miles to the west. There he became one of the legends of the south shore, leading his crews on numerous heroic rescues. He also continued to have dreams that foretold of other wrecks. But they are the grist of other tales.

The Washington Island Light

The waters of Green Bay on Lake Michigan were often filled with small fishing boats, and the loss of one on November 12, 1874, was not especially noteworthy. It was just another small Great Lakes tragedy that would soon be forgotten except for what happened next. The *Sturgeon Bay Expositor* of February 4, 1876, recorded the event.

"A WASHINGTON ISLAND MYSTERY

"Lights floating over the waters of the harbor near where it is supposed two men were drowned and the circumstances connected therewith, as related to us by Mr. E.W. Steward of Washington Island. It will be remembered that in the fall of 1874 two men Halley and Root went out in their fisherman's boat and never returned. The oars, net boxes, etc. coming ashore made it evident they were drowned during a terrible snow storm which arose soon after they went out. This occurred on Thursday, November 12. Some weeks previous to this, on Sunday evening, Halley had an altercation with a neighbor, who struck him with a stone on the head, injuring him so severely that he was partially insane at the time he went out in the boat. It is supposed by the people on the island, that had it not been for Halley's partial insanity, the unfortunate men would have weathered the storm and returned safely to shore. Soon after this disaster, a mysterious light was seen moving along near the ice on Thursday evening, followed again on Sunday evening. These lights appeared during the whole winter regularly on Thursday and Sunday, and occasionally during the summer and have been seen every Thursday and Sunday night during the present winter. The light usually has the appearance of being at the mouth of the Harbor, about a mile to a mile and one-half away. It usually has the appearance of a lantern moving along, about as a man would carry it, sometimes moving along four or five miles, but usually passing back and forth over a space of about a mile near the bluff at the mouth of the Harbor. Sometimes it will appear to flare up and look as large as a basket and again it will rush along at railroad speed for a mile or two. The light is usually pure white with never a halo. Wm. Betts pursued the light one night last winter. He left his house for the purpose, but he was unable to get any nearer than apparently one half to one fourth mile from it, when he went faster the light moved faster and as he slackened his pace the light would follow suit. Finally it turned and moved off toward St. Martin's Island and led him onto such poor ice that he could not follow it further. Now the mystery about this is, its appearance on Thursday and Sunday nights, the one day of the week on which Halley was hurt and the other on which he and his companion were drowned and its being seen in winter mainly when atmospheric lights were not produced by natural causes. Nearly every person on the island has seen it several times and many have seen it dozens of times and there is no doubt of its regular appearance as above stated."[25]

Along the Road

The sleepy old town of Jacobsville is located to the north, just inside the lower entry of the Keweenaw Waterway on Michigan's Keweenaw Peninsula. The town was the site of the original lighthouse marking the waterway's eastern entrance. The first lighthouse was erected in 1856 and, like most of the early lights, was built so poorly it was necessary to replace it. The new lighthouse was built in 1870. Ten years later, a very prosperous quarry started in the area and soon the town of Jacobsville, named after one of the quarry owners, was platted. When the quarry eventually closed, the town gradually became just a shadow of its old self.[26]

Jacobsville's ghost tale involves a deadly lover's triangle and the unexplained disappearance of the three key players. The story was given to me by a local resident and names of the participants have been changed to, as Sgt. Joe Friday on the old "Dragnet" TV series would say, "protect the innocent." Whether the three ended up forever in the cold waters of Keweenaw Bay, buried in a shallow grave in the nearby woods or dropped deep down into the black bottom of an abandoned mine shaft, is unknown. It is a question that likely never will be answered. Wherever they are, the spirit of the cuckolded husband seems to keep returning to Jacobsville again and again! The two lovers, however, have apparently found peace since their ghosts have not been reported.

The 1870 Jacobsville Lighthouse marks the lower entry to the Portage Lake Ship Canal. DONALD L. NELSON PHOTO

91

"Many years ago (I'm guessing around the 1940s), a man named Jones came home early from work one night and found his wife in bed with a lover. After that evening, all three disappeared. Naturally, the speculation was that the husband killed his wife and her lover, then himself. But the husband has been spotted many times walking along the road in Jacobsville near the old Smith residence. When people would take a second glance he'd disappear, literally. He always wore a plaid shirt and jeans and never seemed to age.

"Some of the residents of Jacobsville who claim to have spotted the ghost were Sam Smith, his wife, Minnie, and his father. Sam's brother, who knew nothing of the ghost, saw him on the foggy evening he came to visit Sam and Minnie. The brother was from out of town and Sam and Minnie had picked him up from the airport late at night. It's funny that neither Sam nor Minnie spotted the ghost, but Sam's brother saw him walking down the road near their house. He didn't mention seeing the man until the next morning at the breakfast table, and after describing him, they realized it could be none other than the ghost. Jacobsville is a very small community, and everyone knows everyone and their families. This man fit no other description than that of Mr. Jones.

"Edith Smith's husband, father-in-law, sister and brother Jim had seen the ghost. Edith may be the only one living of that group and the only one in her family who hasn't seen the ghost. Minnie Smith claims that some men were coming out of a sauna one night, spotted the ghost and said hello, whereupon the ghost disappeared into thin air!

"On the morning of my wedding in 1985, one of my husband's relatives took a wrong turn, leading him in the direction where the ghost had been spotted. Realizing that he couldn't find the church and was lost, he stopped and asked a man who was walking on the road for directions. He was given the directions, thanked him and when he looked into the rear view mirror at the man, he was gone. He asked me who he was at the reception, and several of us had no clue, until he mentioned the disappearing act, then we all knew! He then told us the man was wearing a plaid shirt and jeans and, well, you can imagine the shivers we all experienced that warm summer morning!

"As often as I've gone out in the car on a foggy, misty evening searching the road for him, I never saw the ghost. I'm sure it's my strict Baptist upbringing that prevented me from seeing him! Edith Smith claims that he hasn't been seen since Sam Smith's father blessed the area where the ghost lived.

"I'm taking two of my three children camping near Jacobsville this Thursday, and if the weather turns foggy and misty, I know I won't be able to resist getting in the car and driving on the road near the old Jones residence. Maybe now that I'm a Methodist I'll have a chance to see him!"[27]

CHAPTER 4

Shipboard and Underwater Ghosts

Hello Son

Can the dead converse with the living? A particularly chilling ghost story that appeared in the December 15, 1899, issue of the Manistique, Michigan, *Courier* newspaper indicates that it can happen.

"Thanksgiving will ever remain a sad anniversary for the family of Captain W.H. Hargrove, of 897 Trumbull Avenue. Wednesday

Benjamin Hargrove was killed when he fell from the mast of the Ira Owen. *Dossin Great Lakes Museum*

brought to their home the body of their only son, Benjamin L. Hargrove, who on Tuesday last fell 70 feet from the mast of the steambarge *Ira H. Owen,* at Erie, Pa., and died four hours after he struck the deck.

"A few nights later (after the accident), the father, who is captain and owner of the schooner *John Kelderhouse* (and was unaware of his son's death), was passing through the Straits of Mackinac when, through the darkness, he suddenly saw a big barge bearing down on him. It was out of its proper course, but straightened in time to avert an accident. The two boats passed very close to one another and Captain Hargrove was standing at the rail in no amiable mood, when a voice sang out from the other ship.

"Hullow, father, where are you going?" Captain Hargrove recognized his son's voice.

"Chicago," he answered. And then, "How are you, boy?"

"I'm all right," came the reply. "Are you?"

"Yes."

"Good-bye, father. Take care of yourself."

"You do the same. Good-bye."

The son had recognized his father's ship in the distance and bore down on her to exchange greetings, the captain thought.

"When Captain Hargrove arrived at Chicago he found awaiting a telegram announcing his son's death.

"The ill-fated young man, who was 27, was to have been married within a few weeks to a young lady of Belleville, Ontario. He had sent her money to make some purchases for the little home that was to have been theirs, and she was about to carry out his instructions when the news of his death came. The young man was formally a resident of Belleville and was a member of the Belleville lodge F and A."[28]

The Ghost of the *Eliza White*

There is a haunting tale of a ghost on the small Canadian schooner *Eliza White.* Sometime in the early 1900s, the exact time is unknown, the schooner took a load of fertilizer to Hamilton, Ontario, on Lake Ontario. It was early evening when she arrived and after securing his ship to the wharf, the captain went to tell the cargo owner that they had arrived and make arrangements for unloading the cargo. On his way back to the ship, he met one of his crewman running up the road carrying his bag.

When the captain asked where he was going, the sailor answered, "I'm quitting! I wouldn't spend the night aboard that vessel if you gave me her and this trip's freight to boot."

When the captain asked what had happened, the sailor said, "Why, I was sitting smoking in the cabin after you left. All at once a woman in white walked through the room. She looked right at me and the look in her big black eyes froze me fast to the chair. I've never seen such horror and terror and fear and pain. And all the time she kept wringing her hands with the most awful motion, as if her fingers had turned to live snakes!"

The captain tried to argue with him, but to no avail. He knew the sailor was not a drinking man, so it wasn't a case of the d.t.'s. Left with no choice, the captain paid him off.

The strange apparition never appeared again aboard the *Eliza White,* or at least no one ever admitted it did. Was the ghost the result of a murder committed in the cabin a long time before? Was it just a wandering spirit searching for some unknown object or person? The mystery was never solved.[29]

The Westmoreland's Gamblers

One of the earliest underwater ghost tales involves the steamer *Westmoreland,* lost in Lake Michigan's Manitou Passage on December 7, 1854. The big steamer was bound for Mackinac Island with a cargo of winter supplies, including a large amount of liquor and, as legend claims, $100,000 in gold. Ravaged by a terrible storm, the vessel grew top-heavy with ice and foundered somewhere in the passage, taking 17 people down with her.

Because of the rumored gold aboard, she became a much sought after wreck by divers through the years. Reportedly she has been located several times, but the discovery has never been admitted or proven. There are still divers who stand on top of the Sleeping Bear Dunes and look out into the passage, muttering to themselves about finding the old *Westmoreland.*

There is a wonderful tale that soon after the loss, the wreck was found by salvagers, who promptly put a hard hat diver down on her. He reported the vessel sitting upright and relatively undamaged. Working his way into one of the cabins, he discovered half a dozen lumberjacks still seated around a table playing cards. Their stack of coins was still in the center of the table and each man's grub still in front of him. Several of the jacks clutched cards in their hoary hands. Evidently the men were damned if the storm would stop their poker game! The diver closed the door and left, never finding the gold cargo nor checking to see who had the winning hand.[30]

Prins Willem's Divers

In the early evening of October 14, 1954, about four miles off Milwaukee, Wisconsin, in Lake Michigan, the 258-foot Dutch freighter *Prins Willem II* collided with a tug-barge combination. The resulting crash tore a huge 20-foot-by-8-foot hole in the freighter, flooding her engine room. Mortally wounded, the *Prins Willem II* continued on for two more miles before sinking bow first. All 30 crew members safely escaped in lifeboats. The *Prins Willem's* infamous reputation is not the result of her collision loss, but rather the number of divers killed while exploring her. To my knowledge, more divers have been killed on her than any other Great Lakes wreck. The first died in 1985, second in 1989, third in 1992 and fourth in 1997. She has proven herself to be a very deadly underwater encounter.

The following story was related to me a couple of years ago over a few beers at a dive show. Whether it is true or false is unknown. In that regard, diving stories can be a lot like fishing stories. But the diver who related it was most earnest and believable.

"Man, that one scares me! It did the first time I dove it and it still does! It's a hell of a dive, lots of stuff to look at and explore, but after my last dive I don't think I'm going back. Look, I haven't told this to anyone before and I don't want my name used, but the last time was

The wreck of the Prins Willem *has been a death trap for divers.* AUTHOR'S COLLECTION

really weird. The second I hit her at about 40 feet I started to hear voices. I couldn't be sure what they were, it was kind of muffled like someone's talking and you can't quite make out what they are saying.

"Visibility was pretty good, 10 feet or so, and I looked at my buddy. He looked all right, so I gave him the okay sign and we headed back for the engine room. There's lots of good stuff there, especially tools. All the way back the voices kept fading in and out. But I still couldn't make out any words.

"We started down into the engine room and it got black fast. We both switched our lights on and kept moving down. I was leading, my buddy swimming behind me. The whole wreck is knocked over on a 45 degree angle so it is disorienting but not too bad. By the time I got to the engine room I had lost my buddy. He must have stopped to look at something.

"Since we both had been on the *Willy* many times, I figured he would meet me in a few minutes. I was still hearing the voices, but still couldn't make them out. When I finally reached the engine room door, I gave a last look back for my buddy, didn't see him anywhere and I went on in.

"I was looking around in a corner when I had this feeling I wasn't alone. I could feel someone else. I figured it was my missing buddy, so I turned around, but no one was there. Everything is black in there, so I would easily have seen his light. I swung my light around and still there was nothing.

"Then I saw it. Just above the engine there was a diver just kind of floating there. It wasn't my buddy. I don't know who it was. I didn't see another boat when we tied up. The voices suddenly became louder and very clear, 'Get out, Get out!'

"The diver I was looking at was not solid either. My light went right through him. I have never seen a ghost and up to now thought it was all BS. Well it isn't! The diver started to move, slowly finning his way past the engine and right through the wall and out of the engine room. I said, 'I'm out of here.'

"As I was swimming up the companionway toward the deck, I saw another ghost diver looking around a cabin door. I kept going. Once I reached the main deck, I thought I saw another moving to my left. Now I was really rattled, right on the edge of panic.

"My buddy was waiting at the anchor line and I calmed down a bit. When we got back to the boat, I asked where he had been. He said he stopped for a minute on the way to the engine room to look at something. When he turned back to continue, he briefly saw a diver heading up and around the corner. Thinking it was me and something was wrong, he followed, but lost him in the gloom. When he got to the deck, he continued on to the anchor line, figuring that he'd meet me there whatever happened. Other than that he had seen nothing. I didn't tell him what I saw!"[31]

Lost Wreck

We are all familiar with stories of ghost ships that appear briefly enough to be sighted, then quickly disappear. On the lakes the *Chicora, Alpena* and *Bannockburn* all fit into this "Flying Dutchman" category. There seems to be an underwater variation of this experience. For example, in some cases scuba divers have reported finding a wreck only to return later and be unable to relocate it. This brings into question whether it was even there in the first place. What did they really see?

A case in point is the mystery schooner of the Pictured Rocks, just east of Munising, Michigan, on Lake Superior. The story goes that in the late 1950s, when scuba diving was just becoming popular, several area men took up the sport. Knowing the old tales of local shipwrecks, they started diving where they thought the wrecks should be. After a while, their efforts were successful, finding many of the wrecks that divers explore today as part of the Alger Underwater Preserve.

The divers continued to search for new wrecks. It is said that they found a schooner, fully intact less masts, and it was resting in a rock canyon just off the Pictured Rocks. As the tale went, two divers were swimming along the rocky bottom when they came up to the lip of the canyon and looked down into the murky depths. Before them, another 30 or so feet down, was the ship, nestled in as tight as a car in a garage.

It was so well hidden, it could only be seen from almost directly above. Dropping down, they briefly looked the wreck over before the telltale, hard breathing indicated they were coming to the end of their air tanks. This was well before the days of underwater pressure gauges. After one last look at their magnificent find, both men surfaced and returned to their boat.

Although they were confident they could easily find the wreck again, they never did! Regardless of how much they searched, the schooner in the canyon remained lost. The real question is not where it is, but was it ever there to begin with? Was it, in effect, an underwater ghost ship, kind of a sunken *Bannockburn* of the Pictured Rocks? This type of experience has occurred to other divers in other lakes. A wreck is found, then lost. Was the wreck ever there at all?[32]

CHAPTER 5

Hoodoos

The *Comet*

The old lake sailors thought the *Comet* was a hard luck ship. The 174-foot side-wheeler was en route from Kingston, Ontario, to Toronto on May 31, 1861, when she collided with the schooner *Exchange* near Nine Mile Point, Lake Ontario. The schooner received only minor injuries, but the *Comet* was mortally wounded and sank in 40 feet of water.

Reporting the loss, The *Oswego Commercial Times,* commented, "A strange fatality has attended the *Comet* ever since her construction, some 16 years ago. She became noted for accidents, and her passengers and freight were never secure. Her machinery was so often 'on the break,' or the vessel herself on a shoal that the public grew to distrust and avoid her. Finally in 1851, she blew up in our harbor and the terrible scene is yet fresh in the memories of those who witnessed it. If we remember rightly, 11 lives were lost at the explosion. Afterward, she was overhauled, refitted and rechristened and, with the name of the *Mayflower,* drove for many years a prosperous business on the lakes.

"Only a short time since, needing slight repairs, occasion was taken to give her the old name again. She had worn it but a few days when she broke from her moorings in Kingston harbor and sustained damages to the amount of several hundred dollars; and now she closes the list by being sunk. Her loss at this time is about $20,000. She is said to be fully insured."

Comet has not proven to be a lucky name for other vessels, either. At least seven ships carrying the name – steamers, schooners and tugs – came to grief on the Great Lakes. It must also be noted that her name was changed twice, violating another superstition.[33]

The Cursed *Minch*

If one chooses to believe in such things, a strong case can be made that the steamer *Anna C. Minch* was a cursed vessel. Launched in 1903 by the American Shipbuilding Company, she was named for the daughter of a Great Lakes ship owner.

Throughout a career, every freighter goes through any number of bumps and scrapes, the price of working the hard lakes trade. But right from the start, the *Minch* had more than expected and superstitious sailors considered her a hoodoo.

In the years between April 1907 and December 1925, she was involved in six serious collisions with other vessels and an equal number with piers and docks. She grounded three times and was damaged by ice once. In 1925, she stranded on Fox Point Shoals, 15 miles south of Port Washington, Wisconsin, on Lake Michigan. Enough was enough and she was sold to the Western Navigation Company of Fort William, Ontario, in 1926. Under her new colors she ran mostly in the Canadian grain trade. Minor mishaps continued.

The end for the unlucky ship came during the infamous 1940 Armistice Day storm. For reasons unknown, she foundered with all hands off Pentwater, Michigan, in Lake Michigan. When divers found the wreck in 40 feet of water, they discovered a large hole in the bow, the heavy steel smashed in by some great force.

For many years it was believed that the *Minch* had collided with the steamer *William B. Davock,* also lost in the same area during the storm. But when the *Davock* was finally found in 1972,

Sailors thought the Anna C. Minch *was cursed.* AUTHOR'S COLLECTION

she had no evidence of a collision. So what had struck the cursed *Minch,* finally taking her to the grave?[34]

Northern Queen – **Ship Killer**

Can a ship have a malevolence – a sort of evil spirit that inhabits its very hull – making it into a ship killer? If so, the Northern Transportation Company steamer *Northern Queen* would be a prime example. When launched in Cleveland in 1889, there was nothing to suggest an ill-starred career for this 300-foot steel vessel. By all rights, she should have had a long, profitable and uneventful life. It wasn't to be.

Her first victim was the three-masted schooner *Fayette Brown,* cut down on Lake Erie in 1891. When the steamer's steel prow smashed into the soft wood of the schooner, one of the *Brown's* men had the presence of mind to jump to the steamer's fore deck. The rest ended up clinging to the mast tops when the schooner sank to the bottom.

In November, 1908, *Northern Queen* cut down the steamer *North Star,* her own fleet mate, in the fog off Port Sanilac, Michigan, Lake Huron! It was probably a fitting end for the *North Star,* because she was a ship killer herself! In June 1884, she sank the steamer *C.J. Sheffield* off Whitefish Point in Lake Superior. Two months before her "meeting" with the *Northern Queen,* she rammed the steamer *William G. Pollock* off Point Iroquois, also on Lake Superior.

Four years later, the *Northern Queen* cut into the steamer *G.J. Grammar* off Corsich Shoals, Lake Huron, sending her to the bottom of the lake.

The **Northern Queen** *was known as a ship killer.* C. PATRICK LABADIE

The *Northern Queen* led a charmed life concerning her own mortality, surviving the great 1913 hurricane that sank so many bigger and stronger vessels. She was driven aground by the storm on Kettle Point on the Canadian side of Lake Huron but hauled off to sail again. Eventually she went salt water before being cut for scrap in 1925.

By the way, just to add a little superstition to the whole story, there are 13 letters to *Northern Queen!*[35]

The *Fleetwing* Couldn't Outrun Her Luck

Fleetwing is another name that wears a curse.

In December 1866, the schooner-yacht *Fleetwing* raced with two other vessels across the Atlantic as part of a $10,000 challenge match. The other two came through safely. It was different for the *Fleetwing*. In mid-ocean, a rogue wave swept into her cockpit and washed six men overboard to their deaths.

In 1863, the 108-foot schooner *Fleetwing* was built on the American side of Lake Ontario. When nearly new, she was struck by a sudden squall and knocked over, drowning the captain's wife, 5-year-old son and the woman cook. Since she was without cargo, the *Fleetwing* floated and was eventually salvaged. The wife's body was found trapped in a lower bunk in the cabin and that of the son washed ashore at Salmon Point, New York. He still wore the sailor suit his mother had lovingly made for him. The old cook's body was found near Whitby, Ontario, one hand still gripping an old butcher knife.

Repaired and returned to service, old time sailors thought the *Fleetwing* always carried with her the stigma of death. In April 1893, she was bound for Kingston with Oswego coal. The weather was terribly cold and the old schooner was thickly coated with ice. It was also an especially black night. When the short-handed crew fought to take in a steel stiff sail, one of them lost his footing and slid overboard. Although the yawl was quickly launched, the unfortunate man was gone into the dark forever. He left a young wife at home to mourn his passing. The *Fleetwing* was just a "bad" ship. Too many things went wrong with her.

Another *Fleetwing,* a 136-foot schooner, went ashore at Death's Door, at the tip of Wisconsin's Door Peninsula in September 1867, a total loss. The small, 60-ton wooden ferry *Fleetwing* burned and sank in Conneaut harbor in 1920.

In theory, *Fleetwing* is a wonderful name for a vessel, but it has proven to be an unlucky one![36]

The 13th Ship

Superstition always played a strong role in an old time sailor's life. Some superstitions were unique to the profession, like rats and cats aboard a ship. Others were general to the population at large – for example, bad luck associated with the number 13.

Captain William Bonnah of Toledo, Ohio, had sailed the Great Lakes a long time and owned and mastered many vessels. It wasn't until he looked back on his career that he realized that the schooner he was in the process of buying was his 13th and that the date he had scheduled to close the deal was March 13th! He couldn't change the fact that it would be his 13th ship, but he could change the date for closing the deal, shifting it to the next day, just to be on the safe side.

Bonnah must have thought he cheated the 13th superstition, since all was peaceful for four months. Nothing marred the effective operation of his new schooner, the *John Schuette*. On July 2, 1909, fate called in its marker. The schooner was upbound in the Detroit River from Cleveland, Ohio, with a cargo of coal. She was just passing Ecorse, Michigan, at 7 p.m. when a squall knocked her off course. Bonnah and his crew struggled to bring the ship back on track, but it wasn't a quick process for a heavily loaded vessel. They took too long and the *Schuette* drifted across the course of the big excursion steamer *Columbia*. She was coming back from Bois Blanc Island and her decks were crowed with an estimated 2,500 Presbyterian Sunday School picnickers. The *Columbia* easily swung clear of the schooner and continued on up river. The steamer *Alfred Mitchell*, however, was close behind the *Columbia* and partially blinded by her smoke. The *Mitchell* drove hard into the old schooner. The *Schuette* sank so quickly that the crew barely had time to launch her yawl and pull to safety. So ended Captain Bonnah's 13th ship![37]

Old *Number 16*

The *Pere Marquette 16* was an infamous railroad ferry hoodoo. Originally christened the *Shenango No. 2,* she was built by the Craig Shipbuilding Company in Toledo in 1895. The wood steamer was 282 feet in length and had three propellers, two aft and one forward.

From the very start of her career she showed an amazing propensity for getting into trouble. Early on she was in ice difficulty on Lake Erie. Major trouble happened on October 20, 1898. She was entering Milwaukee during the very early morning

The **Pere Marquette 16** was an infamous hoodoo. *K.E. Thro Collection*

hours when she inexplicably stopped responding to the helm.
When the captain signaled full *astern* to the engine room, it was
misunderstood and the engines shifted to full *ahead* sending the
steamer crashing into a partially completed grain elevator,
damaging herself and the elevator.

On December 18, 1899, after being sold and renamed
Muskegon, she departed Milwaukee with a full cargo of 26 railroad
cars. Caught in the open lake by a storm, she was blown into the
trough of the waves and punished badly, eventually barely
struggling back to Milwaukee.

Two months later, February 23, 1900, she again left Milwaukee
in good weather only to be overtaken by a roaring norther in mid-
lake. Heavy seas broke her rudder quadrant. Not able to answer her
helm, she was forced into the trough of the waves. The heavy
rolling soon knocked several cars off their tracks. The loose cars
created havoc, smashing into other cars as well as the bulwarks.
After a desperate effort, the crew secured her rudder amidships and
the captain was able to bring her into safety at Racine, Wisconsin,
using only her engines to steer.

Bad luck continued to dog the car ferry. The following May the
Muskegon collided in a Lake Michigan fog with the scow *Silver Lake*
off Manitowoc, Wisconsin. Cut in two by the steamer, the scow
sank with the loss of one life.

On the night of December 21, 1901, she struck a sand bar
attempting to enter Ludington, Michigan, in a storm. The waves
soon broke her back in two, snapping several steam pipes and

seriously burning three of the engine room crew. Driven by the waves against the north pier, the badly damaged steamer sank to the bottom in 16 feet of water. One of the injured men died before the lifesavers were able to rescue them.

In 1906, the steamer was renamed *Pere Marquette 16.* Normally, a change in name is thought to bring bad luck, but in this case what was there to lose?

Despite the 1906 name change, her bad luck continued. On November 22, she went aground at Pestigo, Wisconsin, but suffered no damage. She collided with a scow in the Sturgeon Bay Canal on May 26, 1907. In another collision off Kewaunee, Wisconsin, on June 21, 1907, she damaged the schooner *Rosebud.* On September 20, 1907, she struck the city dock at Waukegan, Illinois. The next month she was disabled off Waukegan and had to be towed to Chicago.

Her end as a ferry came on November 20, 1907. Running south on Lake Michigan she was struck by a powerful north gale and after fighting the mountainous seas was eventually blown into the wave trough. Two of the cars broke loose and in crashing about the car deck, shattered several steam lines knocking out the engines. Dropping her anchors, she tried to ride out the blow. Repeatedly shuddered by the waves, more cars jumped loose, nearly destroying the car deck as they smashed to and fro. As in the February 23, 1900 accident, only the desperate work of the crew brought the engines back on line and allowed her to safely reach Milwaukee. The repairs needed to put the old wooden steamer back in order were too extensive and she was laid up until she could be sold off.

In 1918, she was purchased by the Hammerhill Paper Company and cut down into a steam barge. Renamed *Harriet B.,* on May 3, 1922, she was struck down by the big 504-foot steel steamer *Quincy A. Shaw* in the fog off Two Harbors, Minnesota, in Lake Superior. Within 20 minutes the old ferry dove for the bottom, a hoodoo to the last.[38]

The Jinxed Car Ferry

Another jinxed car ferry was the *Ann Arbor No. 4.* Built by the Globe Iron Works in Cleveland in 1906, the 269-foot ferry was an important part of the Ann Arbor Railroad link across Lake Michigan. She suffered misfortune after misfortune in a career as troubled as the *Pere Marquette 16.* Some old sailors claimed that she had an accident for every year she sailed.

On January 24, 1909, she ran ashore at Point aux Barques in Lake Michigan. Believing that his vessel was hard aground, the

Sailors also believed the Ann Arbor No. 4 *was unlucky. K.E. THRO COLLECTION*

captain hiked over the ice to shore to wire for a tug. However, once he had trekked out of sight, the wind shifted and the ferry blew free. Imagine his surprise when he returned to discover his boat gone!

While loading in Manistique, Michigan, on October 14, 1909, she suddenly capsized. It took more than a month to right her and salvage costs were considerable.

She ripped off bottom plates on October 14, 1911, while running through the Door Peninsula's Rock Island Passage. Repairs took a month and again were expensive.

On February 12, 1912, *Ann Arbor No. 4* grounded and was badly damaged a mile north of Manitowoc, Wisconsin, while trying to enter the harbor. At the time she was under the command of the first mate, since the captain was attending his brother's wedding.

She went aground during a stiff northeast gale November 18, 1913, on Green Island in Lake Michigan's Green Bay. Damages were slight.

Her worst accident occurred on February 14, 1923. The day before she had departed Frankfort, Michigan, at 8:20 p.m. for Kewaunee, Wisconsin. The seas were calm and a light snow blanketed her in white. Within an hour and a half she was hit by an 80 mph gale. Temperatures plummeted to 20 degrees below zero and heavy ice formed everywhere on the ship. While battling through the cresting seas, a number of her railcars broke loose. Eventually the rolling cars smashed the stern sea gate off, opening her up to disastrous flooding. In a remarkable feat of seamanship, the captain managed to swing her around for a return to Frankfort. He nearly made it back to port. At 7 a.m. on February 14, almost without steerage, he tried to enter the harbor but since his stern was flooded and drawing about five feet more than normal, she struck bottom, shearing off the starboard wheel and rudder stock. When the next wave brought her up, she crashed hard into the south pier. The dying car ferry slowly swung toward the north until she ended up broadside to the pier. After great difficulty the Coast Guard rescued the crew by breeches buoy. Following extensive repairs the car ferry returned to service.

November 28, 1924, saw her aground off Kewaunee, Wisconsin, but with little damage. Grounding again off Kewaunee on February 13, 1925, damage was extensive enough to require a trip to the dry dock.

In 1937, she was sold to the Michigan State Ferries and renamed the *City of Cheboygan*. After converting her railcar deck for autos, she carried traffic over the Straits of Mackinac until the bridge opened in 1958. No longer needed by the state, she was sold and converted to a fish processing plant. In 1974, the old ferry was

The car ferry wrecked while trying to enter the Frankfort, Michigan, harbor.
AUTHOR'S COLLECTION

As the City of Cheboygan, *she was considered a lucky ship.* AUTHOR'S
COLLECTION

finally scraped. It is interesting that as the *Ann Arbor No. 4* she was
considered a hoodoo, lurching from one accident after another, but
as the *City of Cheboygan* she experienced no problems. In her case a
name change did bring good luck instead of bad.[39]

It is also interesting to note that, although it was the *Ann Arbor
No. 4* that got the hoodoo reputation, it's running mate, the *Ann
Arbor No. 5,* had twice the number of accidents. For undetermined
reasons, sailors just never considered her a hoodoo.

The *Northerner*

Another hoodoo was the wooden steamer *Northerner.* Time
and again the vessel was plagued by accident and misfortune.
Among the worst instances: in 1882 she sank the schooner *A.G.
Russell* in a collision in the Soo River with the loss of three lives and
in 1886 she was nearly destroyed by fire at Kelleys Island in Lake
Erie, requiring complete rebuilding.

The 220-foot, 1,136-ton *Northerner* was built in 1871 at
Marine City, Michigan. When finally lost, she was valued at
$50,000 and rated A-2 by Inland Lloyds. Owned by the Rochester
Transportation Company, she was chartered by Ward's Detroit and
Lake Superior Line.

Her end came on December 11, 1892. The *Northerner*
departed Marquette, Michigan, on Lake Superior four days earlier
bound for Port Arthur, Ontario, with a cargo of 3,500 barrels of oil
owned by the Standard Oil Company and 400 tons of railroad
steel. It was to be her last trip of the season. During the night of
December 7, the *Northerner* fetched up on Keweenaw Point.
Whether it was as the result of poor navigation, a faulty compass or
losing her way in a snow squall was never determined. After
jettisoning 2,000 barrels of oil, she was able to free herself from the
reef. Leaking badly, she ran to L'Anse, Michigan, 58 miles to the
south. Initially it was thought that the steamer would winter in
L'Anse but after assessing the damage, the owners ordered her to
sail for Duluth, Minnesota, for repairs and winter lay up.

The Standard Oil Company tried to charter local tugs to
salvage the valuable oil cargo, but all were laid up for the winter
and unavailable. Since the weather was calm, the company felt that
the barrels were probably floating bunched together, making
recovery easy. Area marine men were suspicious. They thought it
was strange that if the steamer was fit to sail to Duluth, she didn't
just go out and recover them herself.

To take charge of the vessel, the underwriters sent Captain
W.H. Rounds of Chicago to L'Anse. In addition, the company sent
Captain John McCullough to relieve the old captain, Peter
McKinnon. McCullough was to bring her to Duluth and would
then sail her the next season.

The *Northerner* was to have left for Duluth on Saturday, but her
engineers refused to go. The same thing happened Sunday. Using all
his persuasive powers to hold the rebellious crew together, Captain
McCullough got them to agree that they would start Monday.

No sooner had the steamer's whistle blown a few minutes after
7 a.m. on Monday, than a fire was discovered raging below decks.
The oil laden vessel was soon completely engulfed by flames.
Unable to save the steamer, the lines were cut and she drifted into
shallow water. By 10 a.m. she had sunk. Burning oil spread out
over the surface of the water and flowed under the dock, nearly
destroying it and a nearby warehouse. Thick, black smoke covered
the whole bay and great spasms of flame shot high into the air. It
was a spectacle few townspeople would forget.

Originally the fire was blamed on a lamp dropped by a
crewman while going down a forward hatch. However, during an
examination of the officers and crew by the local justice of the
peace, arson was strongly suspected. The steward stated there had

been no lights on board for nearly two hours and the claim that the fire started from a dropped lamp was a "blind to cover crookedness."

Marine men thought the fire originated in the lamp room and suspicion fell on the old master, Captain McKinnon. Was he upset enough about being relieved of command to destroy his ship? At the time of the fire, he had not formally relinquished command to the new captain, both having earlier agreed the change would occur after breakfast. In was during breakfast that the blaze was discovered. When the L'Anse Fire Department arrived, Captain McKinnon treated them in what they considered a "peculiar" fashion. As the firemen rushed aboard the burning vessel, he brusquely ordered them off, threatening to "throw them into the lake." Many others thought the *Northerner* was set ablaze by a crewman to avoid making the winter run to Duluth in a leaking and unlucky vessel. Whether burned by captain or crew, the *Northerner*'s luck had finally run out!

Northerner was a decidedly unlucky name. The steamer was the fourth vessel of the same name lost on the lakes. A side-wheeler *Northerner* sank after a collision with the steamer *Forest Queen* on Lake Huron in 1856, with the loss of 12 lives. A bark *Northerner* was lost on Lake Erie in 1861, and a schooner *Northerner* sank off Port Washington on Lake Michigan in 1868. If all vessels with *North* or *Northern* as part of the name are considered, another 20 wrecks can be added to the list.[40]

The year following the *Northerner* loss saw the end of another notorious hoodoo, the steamer *Dean Richmond.* The 1,432-ton, 238-foot vessel, built in Cleveland in 1864 by Quayle and Martin, seemed to blunder from accident to accident. Major misadventures included:

1865 – sunk steamer *Illinois* off Point Pelee, Ohio, after collision

1868 – ashore at Lake Michigan's Grand Traverse Bay

1869 – aground in the St. Clair flats, Michigan

1871 – burned at Mud Lake, Michigan

1874 – ashore at Point Pelee

1878 – collided with schooner off Chicago

1880 – collided with schooner on Lake Michigan.

Her bad luck ended for good on October 14, 1893, when she foundered with all hands in the midst of a screaming Lake Erie gale. Another bad luck boat was gone. As with other black cats, the name itself may have been bad luck. Between 1823 and 1893, three other *Dean Richmonds* were lost on the lakes, as were seven additional vessels with *Richmond* in the name.[41]

The small Canadian schooner *Primrose* was another reported crew killer. Built in Oswego, she was said to have murdered several crews before finally being tamed by a hard driving, no nonsense master.[42]

A strange example of a Lake Ontario curse was the schooner *Jessie L. Breck*. She was one of three vessels, the others being the schooner *Gaskin* and the steamer *McArthur*, that assisted in raising the sunken steamer *Armstrong* in the spring of 1890. Very soon after successfully getting the steamer up, two of the salvage fleet themselves became wrecks. The *Gaskin* went down off Brockville on Lake Ontario, after one of the lifting pontoons stove in her bottom. The *McArthur* later burned to the water's edge at Collins Bay, Ontario. A superstitious sailing poet soon started the jingle, "The *Breck*'s the next." And so she was.

On May 11, 1890, home-bound in a strong gale with timber for Garden Island near Kingston, Ontario, the *Breck* capsized. All eight crewmen aboard drowned. Four of the crew were from a single family! She was actually in sight of port when she went over and many on shore witnessed her tragic end.

While it was evident that the *Breck* rolled during the stress of the weather, there was also a known Jonah aboard. One of the men had been on the schooner *Norway* when the schooner *Bavaria* was lost with all hands and it was exactly the one year anniversary of the disaster. The *Norway* had been one of a string of schooners, including the *Bavaria,* in tow of the steamer *D.D. Calvin.* In the midst of a screaming gale, the *Bavaria* broke loose. Although the *Norway* survived the storm, her crew was considered "tainted" by their proximity to the lost men on the *Bavaria*. Before that, the man considered to be a Jonah crewed in the schooner *Clara White* when she burned. Surely, his association with two shipwrecks proved he was the Jonah behind the lost ships.

The *Breck* was later salvaged and repaired. Renamed the *H.M. Stanley,* she returned to service, but the *Armstrong* curse still gripped her. She later became the tow of the steamer *Africa,* which sank in the fall of 1895, taking all 13 hands down with her. The *Stanley* eventually ended up on the beach at Lyal Island. Was all of this the result of the old curse?[43]

The Canadian steamer *Jack* was another hoodoo. Considered hard to steer and always in trouble, keeping a crew aboard was a constant challenge for her owners.[44]

Hoodoo

Comparatively modern vessels also earned hoodoo status. The whaleback steamer *Henry W. Cort* is a case in point. Built in 1892 by the American Shipbuilding Company at West Superior, Wisconsin, for the Minneapolis, St. Paul and Buffalo Steamship Company, the 320-foot vessel achieved her hoodoo distinction as the result of many mishaps. Originally named the *Pillsbury*, she was sold in 1896 to the Bessemer Steamship Company and renamed *Henry Cort*. With the formation of U.S. Steel in 1901, she passed to the Pittsburgh Steamship Company. From 1901 until 1917, she ran a constant trade of iron ore from the Lake Superior mines down to the mills and coal up for the railroads. In 1906, she reportedly struck the wreck of the ill-fated schooner-barge *Algerian* near Colchester Reef in Lake Erie. It was a precursor of bad luck to come.

When the United States entered World War I in 1917, the need for steel increased and the shipping season was lengthened. The *Cort* had shown itself to be a good ice breaker and, when an early freeze hit, she was sent to western Lake Erie to break ice. Up to this point, she was considered by some sailors to be a lucky ship, despite the name change. Now her luck deserted her.

On December 17, 1917, she was rammed by the steamer *Midvale* and sank in 30 feet of water 4¹/₂ miles from the Colchester Light in Lake Erie. When salvers finally located her on April 24, 1918, she had moved four miles from the place she sank! All the men could reason was that she had no desire to be found, for the lifeless hulk had drifted slowly over the bottom with seven feet of water over her. It took a year's worth of work, four attempts and a large amount of money before she was finally raised to the surface on September 22, 1918, and towed to Toledo, Ohio, for repair. An unfortunate lack of space kept her out of the yard until late fall. Since more work was needed, she was brought to Conneaut, Ohio, to have her deck raised and cabins rebuilt.

In 1927, she was converted into a crane-equipped freighter. A year later while ice breaking, the demons again touched her and she ripped her bottom out for a second time on Colchester Reef. Thinking she was beyond repair, her owners wrote her off to the underwriters, who later sold her to a Detroit firm. In 1933, she holed herself on another reef, sinking to her decks. Again salvage costs were considerable. The following year the *Cort* rammed and sunk a fish tug in Muskegon, Michigan, killing two of the tug's crew.

The end for the unlucky ship came on November 30, 1934, when a 60 mph gale drove her into the rock breakwater at

Muskegon. The mountainous waves eventually broke the *Cort* in two. The 23-man crew was saved by the Coast Guard Cutter *Escanaba,* although one Coast Guardsman lost his life during the rescue. Broken by the wind, waves and rocks, she was finally cut-up for scrap, the end of a Great Lakes hoodoo ship.[45]

The *Griffith*

Could a man have the curse of fire, always being followed by burning and destruction? If so, the captain of the steamer *G.P. Griffith* was certainly a fire Jonah.

Captain Roby of the wooden steamer *G.P. Griffith* was always very careful as far as fire was concerned. He had seen too much of its destruction in his life. When he was younger he had worked in two sawmills that both were destroyed by fire. When he commanded the steamer *Indiana,* she was nearly demolished by fire. Some old sailors likely called him a Jonah. Others said he was just unlucky and his luck could change for the better.

When the *Griffith* was built in Maumee, Ohio, in 1847, special efforts were made to make her as fireproof as possible. The old wooden steamers were notorious firetraps, but the risk could be minimized. David R. Stebbins, a respected engineer, was given a stake in the ship in return for his efforts to assure her fire resistance. A special buffer was provided around her twin smoke stacks to prevent the hot metal from igniting the wood deck, a common source of ignition. Extra space was also included in-between her decks. Both Stebbins and Roby were always looking for ways to prevent fire. For a while all went well. The only fire on the steamer was under her boilers. In the end, their effort failed!

On the night of June 17, 1850, about 20 miles east of Cleveland, Ohio, the *Griffith* caught fire resulting in one of the worst disasters on the Great Lakes. The blaze apparently started deep in the cargo hold. Desperate attempts failed to put out the blaze and Captain Roby headed his ship for shore. The speed of the vessel blew the flames toward the stern, which forced the passengers and crew to crowd to the bow. With no one to feed the boiler fires, the ship slowly lost way.

Captain Roby hoped to slide up on a shallow sandbar near enough to shore that his passengers and crew could safely leave the ship. Instead, she grounded in 7½ feet of water, about 220 yards offshore. Immediately everyone started jumping into the lake to escape the searing heat. In the dark night, many didn't realize how close to shore they really were. Panic reigned everywhere. There was no order. It was everyone for himself. Some people were burned alive. Others drowned in the short stretch of water between ship and beach. One contemporary account said not a woman or child survived except for the wife of the barber. In the morning bodies littered the sandy beach. Captain Roby, his wife, two children and mother were among those lost. Many of the bodies recovered were found to be wearing heavy money belts, the weight of which carried the owners down to their death. Complete passenger lists were unavailable, but it is estimated 250 to 295 people died in the disaster.

A later investigation revealed that the most likely cause of the fire was a quantity of boxed matches in the cargo. A simple shifting of the freight could have started a roaring fire instantly. Did the deadly matches slip by the watchful Captain Roby, perhaps preoccupied with his own family? Was it all a terrible accident, or just the inevitable result of having a fire Jonah as captain?[46]

What Was That?

A UFO

In the late fall of 1993, the 180-foot buoy tender *Sundew* was turning at Devils Island, in the Apostle Islands, outbound from Bayfield, Wisconsin, on Lake Superior, when a most remarkable sight was observed. One of the men on watch remembered the event clearly. "I had the mid-watch, helm/lookout. While on my one-hour lookout, I was startled by four large incandescent-looking lights about two miles out to the east over the islands. I yelled to the con officer (very improperly), 'On the bridge ... what the &*%$# is that?' After a reprimand, the two men who came out, observed this phenomenon. Whatever was attached to the lights

What did the U.S. Coast Guard cutter Sundew *see? AUTHOR'S COLLECTION*

What was the mysterious light that bathed the Amaranth? *U.S. COAST GUARD*

was between 300 and 500 feet long and appeared to rotate, the lights moved to the right. One would drop off and another appeared on the other end. Suddenly it faded out, as if on a giant dimmer switch. The Quarter Master of the Watch and Conning officer thought it was probably pyros or something and passed it off as insignificant. We couldn't see it on radar. About 10 minutes later, two seamen came up on the flying bridge to relieve me and it appeared again off our bow, about five miles out, except stationary at an angle. This time seven of us saw it. I was scared, I'll admit. The captain was awakened and he radioed Group Sault. No experimental aircraft or pyros were out that night, supposedly. The captain said to wake him if it appeared again, for he might have to set general quarters. It never showed up again."

Whatever the men saw that fall night on the wild outer fringe of the Apostle Islands was never determined. In the classic use of the term, it was an "Unidentified Flying Object," or UFO.[47]

Sixty-three years earlier, another government vessel, the lighthouse tender *Amaranth,* had an equally baffling experience. The 156-foot vessel was launched in Cleveland in 1891 and served well until being decommissioned in 1945.

These tough little ships ranged all over the lakes in every kind of weather, executing missions to service the lighthouses and other aids to navigation. Their crews were professional sailors who had "seen it all." Or so they thought!

During the dark night of August 21, 1930, the *Amaranth* was steaming on Lake Superior about 18 miles west of Au Sable Point, Michigan. All was quiet and the vessel in good order. Suddenly a powerful beam of light cut directly over the vessel, just above the tallest mast. The beam appeared to be about 100 feet wide and followed the steamer as she moved through the quiet water. Everyone aboard looked at the strange light in bewilderment. None could even guess at what it was from. It stayed with the ship for an hour then disappeared as suddenly as it came. The men were certain it was not an aberration of the Northern Lights, a phenomenon all were familiar with, nor a beam from the light at Au Sable Point. They were all too knowledgeable about the permutations of lenses and lighthouse beacons to make that error. The incident was reported to district headquarters but they too had no answers. What was the unearthly light?[48]

The buoy tender *Acacia*, a sister ship of the *Sundew*, also had unusual experiences. One of the former crewmen related that they were in two different areas, one on Lake Erie and one on Lake Huron, where the vessel would suffer complete power shut-downs. Everything suddenly just stopped, engines and electricity. After several minutes, whatever had hold of the vessel released it and all was normal again. Every time the vessel reached these areas, the same thing happened! No explanation was ever given for the inexplicable shut-downs.[49]

Another government vessel, the Coast Guard Cutter *Tuscarora*, apparently figured in solving, but not explaining another lake mystery. In a very small article in the *Grand Traverse Herald*, on June 12, 1899, mention was made of the annual "boiling of the bay." It seems that the day before the report, a patch of water in the bay opposite the present-day power plant in west bay literally boiled! After a short period a great geyser of water bolted upward then collapsed back. Shortly afterward, everything quieted back down to a flat calm.

Three years later, a local fisherman drowned in the same area. Some speculated it might have been connected to the boiling phenomenon.

In 1910, the newspaper noted that an excursion boat had become caught in the boil, but none of its two dozen passengers was injured.

The strange boiling water was apparently common enough that everyone knew about it. Generally, it just wasn't newsworthy.

Then the government got involved in the mystery. The *Tuscarora* anchored off the Grand Rapids and Indiana Railroad dock precisely where the water boiled. The *Tuscarora's* normal cruising grounds were lakes Michigan and Superior. Built in

Richmond, Virginia, in 1902, the 178-foot steamer spent most of her early career based out of Milwaukee. Her complement consisted of seven officers and 58 enlisted men. The majority of her time seems to have been spent transporting dignitaries and assisting at various yacht races and civic celebrations. She would be laid-up in the fall and most of the crew discharged until spring when she was placed back on duty and crew hired. With the coming of the European war, she and her crew were transferred to the Navy on April 6, 1917. It was while under Navy control that she made her stop at Traverse City. On September 18 she was sent out of the lakes for duty on the East Coast. She returned in 1920 remaining until 1925, when she returned to the Atlantic to assist in prohibition patrols. The *Tuscarora* was decommissioned in 1936.

Supposedly the *Tuscarora* was in town to tow away a tug. The captain of the cutter, B.L. Reed, told a newspaper editor he would be in the city for a couple of days. When pressed for details, he gave evasive answers.

Intrigued, the newspaper arranged to have men keep an eye on the cutter and her secretive captain. In the dark of the second night their vigilance was rewarded by a remarkable sight. The stern of the

What role did the U.S. Revenue Cutter Tuscarora *play in the boiling of the bay? AUTHOR'S COLLECTION*

steamer bustled with activity and in short order two hard hat divers were dressed, a working stage rigged and the two divers entered the water. The divers were only underwater a short time before they were brought back to the surface and onto the steamer's stern. Nothing could be seen of what they had done or recovered. The *Tuscarora* quickly departed Traverse City without the tug.

The water has never boiled again! What caused the strange boiling? And what did the *Tuscarora* do to stop it? Was this a 1917 version of the infamous Roswell, New Mexico, UFO incident?[50]

The Strange Case of the *Amelia*

Another case of a strange underwater disturbance happened on Lake Michigan at Sylvan Beach in Muskegon, Michigan, on May 2, 1902. The *Detroit Free Press* of May 5, reported the story.

"Bennett & Schnorbach of this city, who have the contract for raising the private launch, *Amelia,* wrecked at Sylvan Beach, say they have a hard job ahead of them. The *Amelia* now stands perfectly upright, only about six feet of its bow being above the surface of the lake. There is now nearly 25 feet of water alongside the boat, and it is 53 feet in length, over 20 feet of its stern is buried in the sand at the bottom of the lake.

"This singular disaster, which occurred last Thursday, was caused by a mysterious subsidence of the bottom of the lake, which phenomenon was accompanied by such a precipitous rush of water as to uptilt the *Amelia* and bury its stern in the bottom of the lake. Whether this occurrence was due to a sudden caving in of a subterranean channel, or an equally mysterious sloughing off of the shore into deeper water, is unknown and will doubtless remain forever an unsolved riddle. In any event, where there was formerly shallow water from three to four feet in depth there is now 18 to 25 feet of water. A portion of the shore 250 feet long and 50 feet back from the water's edge was submerged at the same time. This unusual disaster occurred a short distance south of the Sylvan Beach dock.

"The *Amelia* was sheltered in a boathouse which was built last season at a cost of $1,000, about 100 feet out from the shore. It is elegantly appointed, has a roomy cabin and cost nearly $6,000. It is the property of F.D. Russell of New York City, who owns a cottage and has spent several seasons at Sylvan Beach. The Russells, however, intend to spend the coming summer on the Hudson, and Ives Russell, their son, was at Sylvan Beach at the time, looking after the work of preparing the boat for reshipment to New York.

"So far as is known, the *Amelia* is uninjured except by the damage caused by the water to the engine and interior. It is possible, however, that the piles on which the boathouse rested, in rising to the surface, may have struck the yacht with sufficient force to break a hole in her. The boathouse itself was badly wrecked and had to be cut away from the yacht and floated to a place of safety. The chief difficulty in floating the boat that now presents itself is the fact that 20 feet of its stern are buried in the sand at the bottom of the lake. A strain could not possibly be brought to bear in lifting the boat out without breaking it in two until the sand was worked away from her stern by means of steam jets or a sandsucker."[51]

Was this another strange case of "boiling water?"

Chanting on the Beach

During the summer of 1998, there was a series of reports about a clandestine religious group performing eerie rituals at night on the beach near the Pictured Rocks Miner's Castle on Lake Superior's south shore. One person watching from the bushes saw eight to 10 robed figures dancing and chanting around a bonfire to the beat of low drums. Other observers said they saw small, dead animals on sticks used as part of the ceremony. After a while reports of the strange cultists stopped. The assumption is that they moved to a less inhabited part of the shore. No explanation was ever offered for the mysterious chanters of Miner's Beach.[52]

Where is the Captain?

The crew on the Lake Ontario barge *Hotchkiss* thought their captain, John MacDonald, was acting a bit "peculiar." Friday morning, October 26, 1877, he was nervously pacing his decks, telling his crew he couldn't sleep and was certain he was suffering from some undefined malady. When he went below that afternoon it was the last anyone admitted seeing him. When he didn't come on deck the next morning, the mate pounded on his door. When he did not respond, the man carefully opened the cabin door. He didn't find the captain but did find a large pool of blood on the floor with a stained knife laying in it. A trail of blood led from the cabin, up the companionway and to the rail. Although the ship was thoroughly searched, Captain MacDonald was not found. He had disappeared!

Was it suicide, murder by an unknown assailant or something else? With no other evidence, the coroner ruled suicide. But was it?[53]

Death on the *Miranda*

There is a strange tale in an account of 1871 events concerning the small schooner *Miranda*. Supposedly the schooner was discovered waterlogged on Lake Michigan by another vessel. When the crew boarded her, they found that her yawl was still on the davits, but there was no crew aboard. Searching the ship, they discovered the drowned bodies of an old man and young boy washing around in the flooded cabin.

What had happened to the schooner? Where was the crew? And what happened to the man and boy? There were questions, but no answers.[54]

The People Who Were Not There

Sometimes things are seen that are not really there, or are they? In early January 1999, a resident of Estral Beach, Michigan, on Lake Erie saw what he thought were nine fishermen marooned on a piece of drifting ice. They were waving their arms as if calling for help. Other people on shore also claimed to have seen the figures, although reports of the number of figures varied.

Aware of the dangers the stranded fishermen faced, the Coast Guard, local fire departments and the sheriff departments were notified. A careful search was made, but nothing was found on the ice. Nor was there evidence of anyone having been there. The Coast Guard also said the ice was too thin for anyone to even walk on.

So what was seen? While one person may have made a mistake, mis-identifying birds for humans, would multiple observers from different locations make the same error. What did they really see?[55]

Grand Island's Cloud

At the north end of Lake Superior's Grand Island is a lonely lighthouse high on a rock cliff. Built in 1867, to help ships navigate the treacherous south shore of Lake Superior, the lighthouse has been the scene of several mysteries, including the possible murder of the assistant keeper by the keeper in 1908. Indeed, the old lighthouse has witnessed many strange things, but the most bizarre of all may have been the strange black cloud. On July 27, 1872, keeper William Cameron noted the inexplicable event in his logbook.

"Although it is out of place, in not having received this book before the 18th, I think it well to mention that on the 12th of this month, a dark body appeared in the sky about southeast from this light at 10:40 a.m. I kept my eyes upon it thinking that it was the

Grand Island Lighthouse. AUTHOR'S COLLECTION

blackest thundercloud I have ever seen. All of a sudden, a tremendous flame burst from this dark opaque body and (it) left (an) hour and a half after the explosion. At 11:10, we heard a noise similar to the report of a thousand big guns. The sky was perfectly serene and clear at the time."

What did the keeper see? Some people would say it seemed suspiciously like a rocket as launched from present day Cape Kennedy – but in 1872?[56]

Wave Ho!

As evidenced by the Grand Island keeper's mysterious cloud, lighthouse keepers sometimes did see bizarre things. On February 18, 1880, keeper A.J. Fargo at Lake Ontario's Presque Isle Lighthouse saw a most unusual phenomenon and duly recorded it in his logbook.

"There was observed at this station this morning about 8 o'clock something very singular and wonderful. The wind was blowing off land, quite fresh and been for a day or so and of course there was no sea or breakers of any account on this shore. Suddenly, without any apparent cause, there arose some distance out in the lake, a huge wall of foam, white as snow and unbroken as far as could be seen. And backed up rather followed by a solid mass of

123

water not less than 10 or 12 feet high coming toward the shore like a race horse and with a roar that cannot be described.

"On the edge of the beach was a row of ice banks three or four feet higher than the average height of the water. There was also a much larger row of ice banks 100 feet farther out in the lake, on a sand bar, that was from 10 to 15 feet high. And the same across the space of the two banks of ice was also full of ice.

"When this wave struck these ice banks, it lifted them bodily and carried them back towards the beach, some to rest on the smaller row of banks and others to be broken in pieces and carried from 100 to 200 feet farther back on the beach.

"There was no similar move afterwards. It was raining a little at the time it happened. Something similar happened in the summer of 1876. The lake was very calm, sky clear or light clouds, wind off land very light, when there were heavy waves immediately following each other from the lake and ran back up on an inclined beach about 100 feet."[57]

What caused the unusual wave was never explained. It could have been the result of an earthquake, perhaps in the north country of Canada, but there is no record of such a disturbance. Perhaps it was just as the ancient Lake Superior Indians might conclude, from the swish of the tail of a giant sturgeon!

CHAPTER 7

Other Things

A Tale of Two Ships and One Man

It has always been said that lightning will never strike the same place twice. Well maybe so, but bad luck can strike again and again.

On November 22, 1919, the 180-foot wooden steamer *Myron* was downbound on Lake Superior from Munising, Michigan, with a full load of lumber. Walter R. Neal was her captain. Behind, she towed the schooner-barge *Miztec,* also laden with lumber. About two hours out, both vessels were slammed by a vicious northwest storm. Stressed by the rising seas, the seams on both vessels likely opened, streaming water into the holds. Waves climbing the decks

Captain Neal mastered the Myron *on that last fatal trip. K.E. THRO COLLECTION*

poured more water into the holds. The pumps could not keep up with the flood. Less and less were the ships able to rise to the challenge of the seas. Seeing the pair in deep trouble, the master of the big steel steamer *Adriatic* ran as close to the pair as he dared in an effort to use his bulk to shield them from the worst of the storm.

Off Vermilion Point, Michigan, Neal realized that the strain of towing the *Miztec* was too great, so he cut her loose. The barge promptly dropped her anchor causing the bow to swing into the waves. Although battered, she survived the storm.

The steamer, with Neal at the wheel, continued doggedly on for Whitefish Point. From the watch tower the surfman at the Vermilion Point Coast Guard Station saw the steamer's trouble and sounded the alarm. The crew promptly launched their surfboat and raced for the steamer. The Coast Guardsmen chased her for seven miles but never reached her in time. About a mile and a half northwest of Whitefish Point, the flooding water drowned her boiler fires and the steamer dove for the bottom.

The crew, except for Captain Neal, quickly launched both lifeboats and jumped in. They were doomed anyway. When the steamer sank, all of the lumber cargo piled high on her deck broke loose, surrounding both of the boats with a crashing, heaving mass of heavy timber. The crew was trapped inside a wooden circle of death! The captain of the *Adriatic* tried to break through the flotsam to the men with his ship, but touched bottom twice and was forced to give up the effort.

Meanwhile the 520-foot steel steamer *H.P. Lawrence* had arrived on the scene and, seeing the *Adriatic's* failure, also tried to break in. She was able to push far enough through the wreckage field to be able to throw lines to the men in the boats. But by now it was too late. The men were too frozen to be able to handle them. The lines slipped uselessly through their stiff fingers. When the Coast Guard boat arrived, they too could not get to the men. When the bodies were eventually recovered, they were frozen into grotesque shapes. Some had to be thawed out by a roaring fire so they could be straightened out enough to fit into a coffin! Seventeen men perished with the steamer.

Captain Neal was the only survivor of the disaster. He was in the pilothouse when the steamer started to sink. During the ensuing confusion, it broke free of the hull. Neal quickly climbed out a window and up to the roof where he grimly hung on for a day and a half. Eventually he was rescued off Ile Parisienne, Ontario, by the steamer *W.C. Franz.*

The story now jumps forward to May 14, 1921. The 202-foot wooden steamer *Zillah* is upbound for Duluth, Minnesota, towing the schooner-barges *Pestigo* and *Miztec*. Remember, the *Miztec* was the survivor of the *Myron* sinking. The *Zillah* and the *Miztec* carried salt cargos, while the *Pestigo* was empty.

About 10 miles west of Whitefish Point, the small fleet ran dead into a powerful spring gale. Deciding to run back to the lee of Whitefish Point, the captain of the *Zillah* tried to come around, but in the process the towline to the two barges broke. He left them to their own and continued on alone, arriving safely behind the point a couple of hours later.

The *Pestigo* hoisted a short set of sails and tried to follow the steamer's lead, but the gale was too powerful. With her canvas in tatters, she eventually anchored off Vermilion Point to try to ride out the storm. When it looked like she was going to drag into the offshore bar and go to pieces, the Vermilion Point Coast Guard tried to launch a surfboat to take off the crew. Two of their boats were wrecked during their attempts to launch them from the beach and they had to watch the drama unfold without being able to help. By a miracle the barge's anchors caught at the last minute and she survived.

The *Miztec* had no luck left, apparently having used hers up two years before. She foundered about three miles offshore, taking all seven hands to their death!

There are two coincidences about these disasters that make one seriously question the power of the fates. The *Miztec* sank very close

The Zillah *tried to rescue the crew without success.* MARINE HISTORICAL COLLECTION OF MILWAUKEE PUBLIC LIBRARY

to where *Myron* perished less than two years before. Was there a bond between these ships stronger than we understand?

The only survivor of the *Myron* was her captain, Walter R. Neal. When the *Miztec* foundered, he was working as her mate! Was there some powerful bond calling Neal to join his dead crew?

The *Zillah* did not escape the fates either. On August 29, 1926, she foundered four miles south of Whitefish Point. The *Pestigo* survived until August 11, 1928, when she broke away from her steamer in a gale and went to pieces off Harbor Beach, Michigan, Lake Huron. What was the common denominator that held all these vessels together?[58]

The Captain's Leg

There are many weird stories of the dead trying to communicate with the living. The strangest of all perhaps is that of the captain's wooden leg. The tale goes something like this. Around the latter part of the last century, perhaps in the mid-1880s, there was a peg-legged lake captain on Lake Huron. He mastered a ship that ran between Port Huron and Alpena.

One terrible night the captain and his ship were caught in a powerful storm. In the midst of the tempest a rogue wave swept over the vessel and washed him into the lake where he disappeared. His body was never recovered. Somehow though, the peg leg came loose and washed ashore. Since the captain's initials were carved into the wood, it was eventually returned to the grieving widow and son. She in turn had a special rack made and the leg was proudly displayed over the fireplace mantel.

For a year the peg-leg rested peacefully in its place of honor until the anniversary of the wreck when another big storm blew up. In the middle of the night, a strange rattling noise was heard by the young son. The boy took a candle and went to investigate. He could find nothing amiss in the house, all the windows were tight and doors locked. When he glanced at the fireplace, however, he noticed the peg-leg was shivering. For three or four minutes the bizarre movement persisted. The son could see no reason for it. He reluctantly concluded that it was his father's spirit borne on the wind of the storm. The son went into his mother's room and related what he had seen. She said she had been dreaming of her husband and concluded it was his spirit coming to summon her to the world beyond.

Within several days, the woman was dead. The peg-leg was buried with the woman, the son feeling that if the leg had been the father's method of contacting his wife, it should go with her.[59]

Doc

There are many strange stories of shipwreck and survival on the Great Lakes. Perhaps none is more bizarre than that of Dennis Hale of the *Daniel J. Morrell.*

"I told you not to eat the ice off the peacoat. If you do it will lower your body temperature and you will die!" Hale looked up at the strange figure of a man floating above him and silently obeyed. Then he collapsed back on the raft.

The last major shipwreck before the *Edmund Fitzgerald* in November 1975 was the 580-foot steamer *Daniel J. Morrell* on Lake Huron on November 28, 1966. The *Morrell* was built in 1906 at West Bay City, Michigan by the Bay City Shipbuilding Company. She was typical of the many ore carriers in service on the lakes.

The big steamer left Mullin's Fuel Dock in Windsor, Ontario, on the Detroit River at 7:30 a.m., November 28, 1966. When she passed under the Blue Water Bridge between Port Huron, Michigan, and Sarnia, Ontario, Lake Huron was being whipped by a rising storm. As the *Morrell* churned her way north, it was hard going and many larger boats had gone to shelter, but the *Morrell* plugged her way north, shouldering aside the big waves.

Watchman Dennis Hale, a young sailor from Ashtabula, Ohio, crawled into his bunk in the forward end and read a book for a

The steamer Daniel J. Morrell. *K.E. THRO COLLECTION*

while. He could hear the waves pounding hard into the steel hull, but it was a sound he heard many times before. About 10 p.m., he turned off his reading light and went to sleep. He had no premonition of events to come.

Hale was suddenly wakened by a loud bang! He tried to turn his light on but there was no power. Searching in the dark he found his life jacket, pulled it on and ran topside.

On the spar deck he and other crewman tried to make sense out of what they were seeing. Looking to the stern, he saw that the *Morrell* had hogged, with the middle of the ship up and the bow and stern down. All lights were off on the bow, making it terribly dark. The stern by contrast was blazing with light. Realizing that he was standing only in his shorts, Hale took a chance and ran back to his cabin. Fumbling again in the dark, he was able to find his pea jacket. Returning to the deck he joined a group of men standing around the life raft between the No. 2 and 3 hatches.

Looking back toward the stern they watched the ship slowly break in two, the steel deck tearing apart with a terrific screeching sound. Great showers of sparks and clouds of steam from broken electric and steam lines added to the surrealistic effect. Finally the stern, still under power and with lights blazing, tore free of the dead forward end. The men looked in amazement and horror as the stern steamed past, plowing its way out into the wild storm.

The next thing Hale remembered, he was struggling in the water. He and three other men finally ended up on the small raft, which was nothing more than two steel pontoons with a rough grating on top. It would keep them above the water, but it provided no shelter from wind or wave.

All the survivors on the raft were in shock and none was thinking too clearly. They broke open the box of flares and fired several off, hoping to attract another vessel. No one saw them.

The waves increased in violence and started to break over the raft. To conserve heat and try to stay out of the cutting wind as much as possible, all of the men lay down on the raft. By chance, Hale was in the middle, protected by other men's bodies. None of the men was properly dressed for the cold and wet. Hale was only in his shorts and pea jacket. One man had on only pajamas, another blue jeans and a sweatshirt. The last man was fully clothed with a short jacket. All wore life jackets.

They were constantly drenched by the cresting waves and viciously attacked by the icy wind and spray. Rescue had to come quickly or not at all. As the long night wore on, Hale alternatively prayed and cursed. The men talked among themselves, but as the cold continued to sap their energy, conversation grew less and less.

By dawn the storm had lessened but two of the men were dead. Later in the afternoon the third man died. Hale and his three dead shipmates continued to ride the small raft. He kept weakening, the terrible cold draining his strength.

All through the next night Hale lay on the raft as it rode the falling seas westward. Eventually it washed up on some rocks, several hundred feet off the Michigan shore, east of Point aux Barques. He had drifted roughly 19 miles from the place the steamer sank. He could see lights on a farmhouse. Hale was too weak to move but maybe he could attract attention somehow. Eagerly, with frozen and fumbling hands, he fitted a flare into the gun and fired it. The gun had broken into two pieces after the first time the men used it, so Hale had to hold the parts together to get it to work. The flare arced high into the black sky and exploded into a brilliant show of colored light. No one saw it. Working as quick as he could, he fired another one. No one saw it either. He yelled and screamed. No one heard him. Too stiff to move, he could only lay helplessly on the raft and watch the house. Eventually the lights winked out. The farmer and his family had gone to bed. The night was terribly cold. The water wasn't washing over the raft anymore, but the awful piercing cold struck deep into his bones. That night he slept in fitful snatches.

The next morning, November 30, the farmhouse lights blinked on. He yelled again. There was no response. So near but yet so far. If only someone would look out on the lake! They had to see him!

It wasn't until 12:15 p.m. on the 30th that the Coast Guard was notified the *Morrell* was overdue. The steamer broke so quick, there was no time for a distress call, thus delaying the Coast Guard search and rescue effort. The first break had severed the power lines to the pilothouse and killed the radios. There was no battery powered backup. During the subsequent official investigation, the Coast Guard estimated that the vessel sank in a mere eight minutes!

During the afternoon, overcome with thirst, Hale started to pick at the ice on his peacoat and put it in his mouth. Then the mysterious specter appeared. In Hale's words, "Hovering above the raft was a man dressed in white. His skin was almost translucent, with a bluish tinge. He had moderately long wavy, white hair and a neatly trimmed mustache. His eyebrows were bushy and his eyes deep-set. I remember his eyes seemed to burn with an incredible intensity."

The figure Hale always referred to as Doc, told him, "Stop eating the ice off your peacoat," then, disappeared into nothing.

After his conversation with the strange visitor, Hale felt himself floating above the raft, then spinning wildly into a bizarre white cloud. He arrived at a large green field when he met his mother and was questioned by a man in white. When he asked about his friends on the *Morrell,* he was sent over a hill where he found the bow of the vessel and his shipmates. As the men watched, the stern arrived and mated with the bow, becoming one ship again. He and his forward end fellows went back to visit their friends on the stern. When the two groups got together, they greeted each other in joyous reunion. Then everyone grew quiet. The men looked at Hale with big sad eyes. One turned to him and said, "It's not your time yet. You have to go back."

Hale was then immersed again in the strange spinning cloud and returned to the raft. Still thirsty, he began to again eat the ice off his peacoat. The mysterious specter again appeared and shook his bony, white finger at Hale, telling him, "I told you not to eat the ice off the peacoat. If you do, you will lower your body temperature and die." Hale stopped eating the ice and lay back on the raft.

Drifting in and out of consciousness, he waited for either rescue or death. Suddenly a Coast Guard helicopter was overhead. It landed next to him, the flight crew loaded him aboard and took him to the Harbor Beach, Michigan, hospital. It was touch and go for Hale for a while. His core body temperature was down to 94 degrees. "Doc" was right. Eating ice would indeed have killed him. A priest also gave him the last rites. He was that close to death.

Hale kept the "Doc" part of his story to himself, afraid of being ridiculed. He didn't speak about it for 20 years.

When the *Morrell* sank 28 of 29 men aboard lost their lives. The steamer was the first major vessel to founder in Lake Huron in 42 years. Ironically, she sank nearly in the same position as the steamer *Clifton,* lost in 1924.[60]

Aviation writer Ernest K. Gann coined the phrase "fate is the hunter" and in the case of Dennis Hale, it surely was. That night Hale was not in fate's sights. Consider:

Of all the ships on the lakes that night, why was it the *Morrell* that snapped in two?

Why did Hale make it back from his quarters with his peacoat without which he surely would have died? Why did he think to go get it at all?

Why did Hale make it onto the life raft when others nearby did not? Why did he end up in the middle of the raft and comparatively protected from the wind? Why did he not perish from the cold? Why did the strange specter visit Hale, and not once but twice? Without his intervention, Hale surely would have died from eating the ice. Who was "Doc?" Was he a reincarnation of the Ancient Mariner of salt-water lore or the spirit of one of the old Point aux Barques lifesaving crew?

Why was Hale the only survivor of 29 men?

Perhaps the only answer is that there must be a muster book up yonder and, if your name is not in it, you will not be called. Fate is indeed the hunter.

Ghouls Along the Coast

Webster's dictionary defines "ghoul" as "a legendary evil being that robs graves and feeds on corpses." Although there are no known examples of the bodies of shipwrecked sailors on the lakes being eaten, there are many citations of coastal inhabitants stripping them of valuables.

When the steamer *Iosco* and her tow, the schooner-barge *Olive Jeanette,* disappeared off Lake Superior's Huron Islands on September 2, 1905, all 27 souls aboard were drowned. Only 15 bodies were eventually recovered, washed ashore along the lonely coast. The captain of the *Iosco,* Nelson Gonyaw, was never found, but a searcher did find marks in the sand indicating that a body had been dragged off into the woods. Since it was well known the captain always carried around $600 to $800 on his person, it was thought that ghouls robbed the body, then lugged it into the woods and buried the evidence.

The same storm cast the big steel steamer *Servona* on Sand Island Shoal, just to the northeast of Sand Island in the Apostle Islands. Several of her crew drowned when their improvised hatch cover raft tumbled over in the surf. Some of the dead were robbed by ghouls from Bayfield, Wisconsin. Charges were filed against several men but were inexplicably dropped.[61]

In one instance, the plundering of a body was done by a lightkeeper. On September 14, 1882, when the big Canadian steamer *Asia* sank in Georgian Bay, 123 men, women and children went down with her. Only two people survived the disaster. In the days following, great efforts were made to recover the bodies for return to their families. One of the vessels involved in the search was the tug *Kendall.* Since it was thought that the *Asia* had perished near Lonely Island in the northwest corner of Georgian Bay, it became one of the first stops. When the captain of the tug asked the lightkeeper if any of the victims had come ashore, he was told, "none." Not believing the keeper, the tug captain asked again more forcefully. Only after a pointed interrogation did the keeper admit that he did find the body of a woman, but she was so badly decomposed he buried her immediately. Feeling the keeper was still hiding the truth, the tug captain demanded to see the grave. What the searchers finally found was the body of a woman near the water's edge with a plank across it. Carefully examining it, they found impressions of a necklace and finger ring. Confronted again by the tug captain, the keeper broke down, telling him that he had taken a pearl broach, some money and a gold watch. A search of the keepers house found numerous other items from the wreck, including stools, chairs, a cabin door, block and tackle and three life preservers. The last had a "disagreeable smell," which led the tug men to believe that they had been on bodies and that more victims were hidden on the island.[62]

Such behavior toward the dead wasn't all that

The steamer Iosco *and schooner-barge* Olive Jeanette *were lost with all hands in September 1905.* K.E. THRO COLLECTION

134

The steamer Servona. *MARINE HISTORICAL COLLECTION OF MILWAUKEE PUBLIC LIBRARY*

unusual. The bodies of shipwreck victims were often considered fair game for all who found them.

A particularly ghoulish story is told of an incident along Lake Superior's infamous shipwreck coast in the area just west of Whitefish Point. It seems that in the 1930s or '40s, two men, one a grizzled old-timer and the other a teen-ager, were hiking the shore just after a strong northwester blew through. The pair found two weathered wooden coffins washed high on the sandy beach. Evidently the waves had undercut an ancient cemetery uncovering the pair and carrying them down the shore. The younger man wanted to stay clear of them, but the older man convinced him to come closer for a better look. Within minutes the old-timer had broken the lids off both boxes. One contained the body of an elderly man dressed in black and wearing a large silver cross. The other held the remains of a woman dressed as an Indian princess complete with native jewelry. Both bodies were badly decayed, more skeleton than anything else. The old man offered the Indian trinkets to the younger man who refused even to touch them, repelled by the very idea of plundering the dead. The older man, however, robbed both of their valuables as a simple matter of course.

Although more common to the Atlantic coast, legend claims there was some "wrecking" activity in the lakes, especially in the Long Point area of Lake Erie. Also known as "blackbirding" or "moon cussing," it involved setting a false light to lure vessels onto the beach or into a reef. One traditional technique involved placing

135

a lantern on a horse's head and leading it along the shore. The uneven motion of the light resembled the action of an anchor light on a moored vessel. Seeing the rocking light, an unsuspecting captain assumed it was another vessel and therefore it was safe for him to run into the same area. When he struck the bar, all was lost.

A procedure used by the Long Point blackbirders involved erecting a false light to deceive ships trying to enter the inner bay. Seeing the light, captains turned too soon and went hard up on the reefs.

The men who set such false lights were the lowest sort of creatures, another variety of ghoul. Some stories told of the wreckers murdering the vessel's crew and passengers. Such tales were enough to cause sailors to flee for their lives as quickly as their vessels struck. The wreckers would then swarm out from shore and steal whatever cargo they could.

Long Point was a wild and desolate place, far from the rule of law. Many terrible things happened on this sandy spit of shore. The heyday of the Long Point wreckers was in the 1840s to the early 1860s. By the end of the middle of the 19th century, legal authority finally reached the point and the ghastly practice of wrecking ended. Today it is the stuff of legend.[63]

After the steamer *G.P. Griffith* burned on Lake Erie in 1850, many of the victims who washed ashore were buried in several mass graves on the beach. A mere five days after the tragedy, people reported that the graves had been opened by ghouls looking for valuables that may have been buried with the victims.

Ghouls had a field day when the *Lady Elgin* sank off Winnetka, Illinois, in 1860. An estimated 300 people perished with her and the local ghouls lost no time in robbing the bodies of valuables as the victims slowly drifted ashore. Several people were arrested for stealing from the dead, but they were the exception.

Lakeshore ghouls struck again in November 1875. On the 15th of the month, the schooner *Fearless* dragged her anchors in a gale and went on a sandbar near Toronto's eastern gap. Believing his ship was going to pieces, Captain William Ferguson made the decision to abandon her in the yawl. His crew lowered it into the water and, holding fast to the painter, brought it close alongside. The captain was the first man into the boat, intending to help when the crew lowered the woman cook into it. In the confusion, the painter was lost and the yawl, with Captain Ferguson, was swept off into the waves and capsized. The captain was drowned.

Without any means to get ashore, the crew took to the rigging, where they lashed themselves tight. The following day, local lifesavers safely removed them, although all were more dead than alive. The captain's body was never found. Marine men thought that if he made it to shore alive, he was murdered by the Brooks Bush gang, a group of beach-combing thugs and the body quickly buried in the shifting sand. It was known that he had $360 of ship's money with him and, later, that infamous gang was seen to be "in the flush." Where might their money have come from, if not the luckless captain?

Previous ghouls stories related how they stole from the bodies of shipwreck victims, but there are genuine cases of cannibalism in the Great Lakes region. In the *Jesuit Relations* there is a story of the Hurons capturing a number of Iroquois, including a Chief Ononkwaya. As was their custom under the circumstances, all of the prisoners were distributed to different Huron villages for torture and feasting.

After being baptized by Jesuit Priests (who were in the village, but could not stop the act to follow), the chief was tied to a stake on a small platform and a low fire built beneath him. The low fire would roast him slowly, providing hours of entertainment for the Hurons. Despite the tremendous pain, the chief never let a cry of anguish escape his lips. He bore the torture stoically, as befit a chief!

When the Hurons thought him dead, they scalped him, only to have him suddenly break from the ropes holding him to the stake, grab a flaming piece of wood and chase them from the platform. For several minutes the bleeding, scorched and battered chief held the shocked Hurons at bay while they in turn threw stones, sticks and clubs at him. When he tripped and fell to the ground the crowd surged in, picked him up and pitched him directly into the wildly dancing flames.

The chief leaped to his feet and, grabbing a flaming piece of wood in each hand, again lashed out at the crowd. The Hurons fell back in terror! When the chief started to run towards the village, evidently with the idea to set it afire, a Huron warrior tripped him. The crowd again leaped on the fallen chief. Now they cut off both hands and feet before throwing him back into the fire. Again the chief emerged from the flames, now crawling on the bloody stumps of his hands and feet, his eyes flashing with revenge and a terrible war cry tearing from his throat. Again the cowed Hurons drew back in fear from the ferocious Iroquois chief.

After gathering their courage, the Hurons finally knocked the crawling chief over, then chopped off his head. Wasting no more time, they quickly feasted on the remains of the brave and courageous enemy. By eating him, they believed that they would acquire part of his bravery. The shocked Jesuits later buried one of the chief's hands.[64]

The great explorer and voyager Etienne Brule met his end in 1633, also a victim of cannibalism. Why he was killed is unknown, but in a lonely Huron village on the north shore of Penetang Bay on Lake Huron, he became the "main course."[65]

During the famine of 1767, fur trader Alexander Henry encountered cannibalism. In the depth of the winter, Henry was sitting at a campfire at Goulais Bay on eastern Lake Superior with his Indian guides and their families. Suddenly an emaciated Indian man appeared at the edge of the firelight. Henry cautiously handed the man a piece of fish but the stranger refused it, quickly turning his head away. The Indian people in the group believed that he was possessed by a Windigo, a terrible spirit that ate human flesh.

When the strange man left, Henry and some of his men followed his tracks until they came to his camp. There they discovered a low campfire and a half eaten hand. When they again offered the man fish, he refused once more. Pressed by questions, the man said that he had killed and eaten his uncle and four children. His wild and ravenous eyes looked hungrily at the children in Henry's group. Believing that once a man tasted human flesh, he would eat nothing else, the Indian men axed the cannibal to death.[66]

Message in a Bottle

Sometimes messages from beyond were unclear as to what wreck they came from. For example, the May 29, 1869, issue of the *Green Bay Advocate* carried a small article about a message in a bottle found in the bay. It was horridly written on an old delivery ticket. "Upset off Washington Island, May 1866, James P. (unintelligible), Frank Hogg, John Nickle." On the reverse was scrawled, "My poor wife. What will she do. Life insured." Although likely from a fishing boat, little else was known about the incident.[67]

One of the victims of the great storm of November 1913 was the schooner-barge *Plymouth*. The barge was in the tow of the tug *James H. Martin,* bound for Search Bay, Michigan, and in the vicinity of Death's Door when the storm slammed into them. Unable to make headway, the tug anchored the barge behind Gull Island, then ran for shelter behind nearby Big Summer Island. When the tug returned for the *Plymouth* the next day, she was gone. The speculation was she broke loose from her anchor and foundered in the open lake. Eventually bodies from her six-man

The schooner Plymouth *was ashore at Marquette, Michigan, on Lake Superior on October 24, 1887. Later she was lost with all hands on Lake Michigan.* AUTHOR'S COLLECTION

crew came ashore near Pentwater, Michigan, along with a note in a bottle from one Christ Keenan, a deputy federal marshal aboard the barge to "secure" it pending legal action against her owners. "Dear wife and children: We were left up here in Lake Michigan by McKinnon, captain of the tug *James H. Martin* at anchor. He went away and never said good-bye or anything to us. Lost one man last night. We have been out in the storm 40 hours. Good-bye dear ones, I might see you in heaven. Pray for me. Christ K. I felt so bad I had another man write for me. Huebel owes $35 so you can get it. Good bye forever."

One of the frustrations of doing the kind of research this book requires is finding material that cannot be properly attributed. Often it takes the form of a yellowed newspaper clipping that has no date or note as to what paper it was clipped from. Sometimes, it is just a sheaf of papers, equally mysterious as to citation. The following piece well fits into this category.

I Alone

"I alone survived the wreck of the brig *H.G. Stamback*. The loss was attributed to the tremendous storm, of course, not what I am going to tell you, but take it from someone who was there. This is the true story of the wreck.

"Before I relate this narrative, I must point out that I was a well educated man, private schools in New England and enough time in one of the old colleges to allow me to successfully read for the law. I was by any standard, a gentlemen. My path in life was set; practice law in my father's firm, a good marriage, a seat or two on a good board, in the end a very comfortable and pleasant life. For inexplicable reasons though, my health began to fail and my physician suggested a trip to the lakes to regain it. His advice worked, perhaps too well. I got on so favorably here, I decided to stay. Eventually I met up with Captain John and took a couple of trips with him on his brig. We got along well enough together that after a while he made me his mate, the position I held when the vessel was lost.

"It was the fall of 1857, and we were at Buffalo. Shipping was down and it looked like the end of the season when the captain was chartered for a trip to Chicago by a woman anxious to get there before winter and not desiring of making the tedious overland journey. As a bonus, the captain also arranged for a partial cargo of barreled whiskey. That's a commodity always in demand and as it was on his account, should fetch a good profit!

"The woman arrived at the dock well after dark in a closed carriage. A considerable amount of baggage accompanied her, including several large trunks, and an unusual chest about five feet long, two feet deep and two feet wide. Since she wanted this in her cabin, a couple of the boys wrestled it in for her. The woman was very finely dressed and a great beauty in a shadowy and mysterious fashion. I'd guess her age about 30 or so, with a very pale, almost white complexion. Her eyes were very dark almost black, and most engaging, nearly hypnotic. From her overall pallor and appearance, however, I would guess her to have been recently ill. The lake trip would be far easier than overland for a woman as delicate as she.

The captain immediately escorted her to her cabin. I noticed she leaned heavily on his arm as he led her below. He never mentioned to me how he had arranged the charter and it certainly wasn't my place to inquire. Within the hour we were under the tow of one of the numerous little harbor tugs that brought us to the harbor mouth and soon after moving under easy sail bound west. We were sailing with a short crew, our regular men having left for their homes or other employment. Other than the captain and myself, there was the cook, an old fellow named Hobbs, I think, a ship's boy and five men forward. As was my job, I obtained the forecastle men from our usual saloon, the bar tender being very adapt at providing our needs. The captain hired on the cook, who had sailed with him before. I found the boy hanging around the saloon and hired him thinking he could be of use helping the passenger. Because of the lateness of the season, a bonus was promised by the captain on arrival in Chicago.

"The first night out everything went well, a good northeast breeze kept us bowling along and I saw nothing of the woman. The breeze was slanting northeast the next day resulting in a sharp chop so it didn't surprise me not to see her all day. The captain and I assumed she was suffering from the sea sickness and decided to stay in her cabin. The cook said he rapped at the door offering some tea and biscuits but received no answer. Later in the day I realized I had not seen the boy about the ship. On my inquiry, neither had the captain, cook or crew. He had just disappeared. Searching the ship failed to find him, so we had to assume he had somehow fallen overboard during the night. For someone unfamiliar with the ways of a ship, such accidents were not uncommon.

"Just after dark she came on deck, looking as beautiful as I remembered from my brief glimpse the previous night. Although somewhat pale, she did appear stronger. She confessed it was as we had surmised, that a touch of the 'mal de mer' kept her confined. At this point the cook came up and inquired if she would like a little late supper, he could put something together for her. She replied that her stomach still was too delicate for food, then walked to the lee rail and just stood there gazing out at the black lake. Her accent was unusual. I had traveled in Europe with my father as a youngster but still could not place it. After a while I went over to her and tried to make a little polite conversation, but she rebuffed me, saying she would rather be alone.

"Wounded, I retreated to my post at the weather rail for awhile, then down to my cabin after leaving orders with the wheelman to call me if the weather changed or anything looked dangerous. About an hour later I was awakened by the violent motion of the ship. She had nearly broached!

"Rushing to the deck just seconds ahead of the captain, I saw the wheelman standing unsteady at the wheel. Cursing him loudly for his inattention, I grabbed the wheel and horsed the ship back around. Had the weather been foul, his error could have been disastrous. The man appeared almost drunk, staggering on his feet and eventually collapsing in a heap on the deck. Two of the boys from forward, also awakened by the motion, carried him to his bunk. Another assumed his trick at the wheel. The woman was no where around, evidently having gone to her cabin before the excitement.

"Dawn the next day found us off Erie and a hard day's sail with the northeasterly breeze brought the ship to Colchester Reef by nightfall. It was a good run for the old girl. The woman continued to stay in her cabin. That night the captain stayed on deck given the dangerous area we were in as he worked her up toward the Detroit River. Later a tug passed us a hawser for the tow up the river. The old man told me the next morning that the woman came up around midnight, said a brief hello to him and then walked forward. The seas were calm enough, so he thought a stroll would be safe. Once she passed the foremast she was too deep in the gloom to be seen. About 10 minutes later she walked back to the stern, passing him without comment and went directly down to her cabin.

"As dawn broke the following morning, the captain saw a man collapsed on the foredeck. Rushing forward the old man immediately saw how pale his skin was and the lethargic look in his eyes. He was taken to his bunk and given a dose of salts from the captain's medicine box. Just after night fall, we dropped the tow, put up our rags and continued out onto Lake Huron. Again the wind was favorable and easy. The woman came up a couple hours afterward and gave no explanation for her absence during the day. She looked much better than the previous night. There was more color on her cheeks and her lips were pleasantly red. The lake air must have agreed with her. She gave me a casual and cold good evening and took her lonely place at the rail.

"The next morning the cook was too ill to make breakfast. When the captain looked him over, it was plain he was not shamming. His skin was ghastly white and eyes dull, as if he was in a trance. These were the same symptoms as the two sick crewman. Captain John told him to lay back in his bunk and take it easy, although I am not certain the man heard a word he said. The rest of the day was uneventful. The winds continued fair and by nightfall we were abeam Thunder Bay Island.

At dusk, the captain went below for what he said was a short nap and never came back topside. When he didn't respond to stomping the deck over his cabin, our usual signal to him his time was up, I went down to check on him. He seemed to have taken sick with whatever malady struck the cook and sailor down. He was dreadfully white and eyes absent all spark. My shaking could not fully waken him. I went back on deck and sent one of the men down to sit with him and to look in on the cook too. Perhaps an hour later, the woman came up for her nightly air. If she was beautiful before, tonight she was positively ravishing! Her skin was flushed pink and full lips literally glowed crimson. Her eyes were more sparkling than previously too. By the pale light of the full moon, she was exquisite. She gave me her cursory cold good evening and retreated to the lee rail. What a shame her personality didn't match her beauty.

"I stayed on deck until 3 a.m., then retreated to my bunk, instructing the watch to call me at dawn. It was a quiet night. When day broke, we were abeam Bois Blanc Island. Sometime during the night, the cook had died. The man who was alternating between the captain and him, had fallen asleep. When he awoke a little past daybreak and belatedly checked the cook, he found him lifeless. He immediately summoned me to the cook's little sleeping corner in the galley. There was no doubt he was stone cold dead. Whatever was striking down the crew was indeed fatal. Most odd was the evident loss of blood. The skin was almost white. Curious, I stuck my knife blade into his arm and there was no bleeding, only the barest hint of redness! This was very strange. I had never heard of any illness that would so destroy the blood. If this was salt water, we would have immediately buried him at sea. On the lakes, such things are not done. We wrapped him tightly in his blanket and carried him to the hold. We would be at Chicago in a few days and he would keep until then.

"The winds turned westerly and it took most of the day to get to the Straits. By the time we came abeam of Old Mission Light, it was well after night fall. Several hours later the woman came up on deck as was by now her habit. By the light of the pale moon, she was as lovely as ever. Short handed as we were with the strange sickness, I told the man at the wheel to get some sleep. I would take his place for a few hours. The woman climbed down the stairs to the deck and started to walk forward. The moon was sliding in and out of the clouds. When it was out I could see the bow. When the clouds obscured it, I had trouble seeing as far as the mainmast. I noticed, though, that she appeared to glide rather than walk. Captured by her face, I had never noticed this before. But with her long, flowing white dress I was certain this was just an illusion. I watched her carefully as she moved toward the bow, then she disappeared from view in the gloom. Ten or so minutes later, she recrossed the deck and descended the stairs to her cabin. Again, she seemed to glide rather than walk, her motion was so graceful.

"The next morning another man was found unconscious on the foredeck. Like the others, his skin was pale and he could not be roused. He, too, was carried to his bunk. The two remaining crewman and I would have a tough time bringing her to Chicago, but we resolved to continue. If the weather held, and the confounded sickness would stay away, we could do it. Then the storm struck! I had seen no warning of it, or any of the traditional weather signs of its approach. In an instant it was on us!

"The first blast blew out the foretopsail. Since we were too short handed to bring it in, that was fine with me. The second burst nearly knocked us over before the mainsail let go followed by the foresail. Only the fore staysail remained and that was only for a few minutes before it too went flying off into the dark. We were now under bare poles. The wind increased by the minute, each gust more powerful than the last. I put both of the remaining healthy hands on the wheel, trying to keep her steady in the overwhelming wind.

"When everything seemed to be under control at least for the moment, I went below to see how the captain and woman passenger were faring. I knocked hard on her door but got no response. Even considering the storm, she should have heard me. I opened the door, an act I as a gentlemen never would have done, except for this emergency. She wasn't there. The box the crew had man-handled into the cabin was laying open on the floor. It was empty except for a thin layer of dirt. This was most strange, but considering the terrible danger we were in, of no immediate concern. Out of the corner of my eye, I saw a leg projecting from behind the trunk. It was the boy and he was very dead. Like the others, he was nearly white. He had not fallen overboard after all. But what was he doing in the woman's room? Next I went to the captain's cabin. When I opened the door, there she was, on her knees bent over him, her slender back toward me. She must have heard the door, but with all the screaming of the wind and creaking of the ship, I'll never know how. She quickly looked up at me. I'll never forget it. Blood was dripping from her lips and her wild, glowing eyes burned with an unholy intensity. Two short white fangs extended down from her mouth. I turned and started to flee from that horrible sight.

At that very moment the ship lurched violently, knocking the woman to the deck and throwing me hard against a bulwark. Being a sailor, I was more used to such extreme motion. I quickly recovered and ran up the companionway to the quarterdeck.

"The two men I had left at the wheel were gone and the wheel itself smashed. Apparently a massive wave had crashed aboard and swept them away. We were rolling wildly, caught in the very jaws of the storm. Thunder rolled overhead and sharp flashes of lightning lit the night sky. Our poles were still up but the strain on them was immense. They could not long last. The ship was doomed as were all of us in her.

"Then the woman struck me from behind with tremendous force, sending me tumbling down the deck and crashing into the mainmast fife rail. Looking up from the deck, I saw her in all her evil. What kind of creature she was, what beast in human form, I do not know. In the cutting wind she was the pure embodiment of the devil. Her white dress, torn and streaked black with the captain's blood, blew stiffly out behind her as did her long black hair. Her eyes flashed red with a blood lust unsated. All this said, there was an evil beauty to her that was undeniable in its power. As she advanced to me over the heaving deck, I was frozen to the rail and could not run, her glaring eyes riveting me to my place. I was caught just as surely as any animal in a leg trap. In that instance I finally realized that she was the cause of the strange sickness and death among the crew. Perhaps the storm was the consequence of the heavens lashing out against her evil!

"When she reached me, her powerful hands grabbed my shoulders and pulled me easily to my feet. Her strength was incredible! She gave a short growl baring her sharp fangs and lifted her head back, preparing to plunge them deep into my neck. Again, I could not move, held as motionless as a statue, as much by fear as by her hold.

"The ship suddenly pitched wildly, breaking her grip and forcing her to step backwards. I held fast to the fife rail. A tremendous clap of thunder boomed overhead and a bolt of lightning shot to the main topmast, shattering it into several pieces. One of them, five or six feet long, fell directly to the deck, impaling the woman through her chest just as Ahab struck the whale.

145

"I watched dumbly as her blood gushed black on the deck, only to be washed immediately away by the rain and wave wash. Mesmerized by the sight, I must have held to the rail for several minutes, watching as her lifeless body drifted to and fro across the deck.

"Then the ship went over, rolling bottom up, and I was thrown into the lake. Fighting my way back to the surface, I grabbed a floating hatch grate and hung on to it. The storm ended very soon after. After six or so hours I came ashore at one of the Manitous.

"I found a farm house where I was given food and sheltered for several days, then hitched a ride on a fish boat to the mainland. I never told the full story of what really happened, only that a violent squall had sunk the ship and I was the only survivor. Who would believe the true story anyway? Considering the time of the year, no one questioned me closely. Old Captain John owned the ship and carried no insurance, so there were no underwriters to satisfy with an endless stream of details. He was a single man, too, and had no family I knew of. The crew was a scratch one, mostly just drifters. In short, no one had any personal interest in what happened to the ship.

The woman, or whatever she was, was dead, killed by the topmast, so she was of no consequence. Later I heard that the hull drifted on a reef off North Manitou Island but soon slipped off into deep water. When I arrived at Buffalo, I gathered my meager gear from my room at the boarding house and went back east. After all, I had recovered my health and, considering the circumstances, had no reason to remain. I spent the last 30-odd years at the law and my end is coming near. Regardless of what anyone may think, I wanted the full story of the loss of the *Stamback* to be a matter of record, official or not. By this date, more than 40 years later, whatever anyone thinks of me, or my senses, is immaterial."[68]

The Mate's Return

This is a yarn, it's hard to say how true it is, about murder and revenge on one of the old steamboats. There is a ghost involved too! A friend of the family told it to me about 25 years ago. He got it from my father's uncle a long time before that. It has certainly been embellished some over the years, but I always thought there was some real fact in it. I didn't write it down at the time nor have I been able to run down all the facts of it, but as I remember, it goes something like this.

The boat in the story ran on Lake Erie between Cleveland and a port on the Canadian side of the lake. She carried both passengers and freight and was a great favorite with the public. Her interior was very fancy, with a big ornate salon, lots of carpet, deep mahogany furniture and paneling, little side cabins for overnight berths, a separate ladies' lounge in the stern and a big gentlemen's smoking room amidships. But it was the cuisine that really set the boat apart from the others on the lake. It was the highlight of every trip. For the noon meal and supper, the boat set a huge buffet of only the best victuals available. A bar provided both hard liquor and fine wines. As I said, it was a very fancy boat and very popular.

Her captain wasn't much of a real sailor. But he was a smooth talker and superb with the passengers, able to convince even seasick travelers what a great time they were having. He kept everyone happy and smiling and all were sure to sail again with him. He especially charmed the ladies. Not only the ones aboard, but also ashore. The wags said like all sailors, he had a wife in every port. By any account he was a rake of the first order, with the motto, "love 'em and leave 'em." His personal life was a series of promises unkept, at least concerning females. The ship's owners were aware of the captain's shortcomings as a seaman and to help make up for it, hired an especially competent mate. He kept things shipshape while the captain played the politician. The owners were not concerned with the captain's personal transgressions as long as it didn't affect the boat's profitability.

Everyone who knew him said the mate was an honest, hardworking sailor man. Eventually he fell in love with and married a beautiful girl from his hometown, a small village some miles south of Cleveland. She was much younger than he was, but when two people are in love, the age difference is not a concern. Rather than leave her alone in the big city when he went sailing, he used his position to get her a job as a stewardess on his ship. He thought this way he could keep an eye on her, plus they could have a little extra money to buy the small farm they had often spoken of settling down to.

For a while, everything was wonderful. The long summer days were idyllic. As the boat plied the steady run back and forth across the lake, there was ample opportunity for the newlyweds to enjoy each other's company. Toward the end of summer though, the captain took notice of his mate's comely wife. When the mate was otherwise employed, he paid little compliments to her. He went out of his way to praise her work, as well as how pretty she looked every morning. He used his considerable skill to slowly and methodically seduce her as he had so many women before. For the captain it was the thrill of the hunt. Once the conquest was achieved, the woman, old or young, beautiful or homely, maid or married, held little interest for him.

The mate was a loyal and good husband, but when the captain turned his charm on, there was no comparison. The young wife was completely smitten by the dashing and handsome master. He used his position to keep the mate busy elsewhere while he and the young wife dallied in his cabin. Of course, as is normal in such circumstances, everyone on the boat knew what was going on but the mate. Eventually one of the crew finally told the man of the sad affair.

That night the mate confronted his wife with the allegation. Brazenly she admitted it, saying she would rather be the captain's woman than the mate's wife. The mate was struck dumb with her infidelity. She quickly ran off to the captain's cabin and did not return.

In the cold light of morning the captain realized he may have made another conquest, but he had also made a terrible mistake. By taking the mate's wife, the man was sure to leave the boat when they got back to Cleveland and when the owners found out the cause, there would be repercussions, especially since the mate was the brother-in-law of one of the owners. Regardless of the captain's diplomatic skills with the passengers, the insult he committed would assure his dismissal. In his unbalanced mind he determined that the only solution was to get rid of the mate before they returned to Cleveland.

Shortly after departing the Canadian shore, a strong fall storm swept over the lake. It would be a heavy weather run back to Cleveland, a real dirty trip. It was the last run of the season and they carried no passengers, only freight.

All day long the captain continued to brood over his problem. Even the woman's ministrations couldn't pull him out of his black mood. Finally he reached his decision and steeled himself to do what he thought must be done. About two hours out from Cleveland, the storm reached a crescendo of violence. The night was black as sin and waves battered at the steamer thunderously. The mate was at his place in the pilothouse, keeping the wheelman steady in the face of the powerful seas. The boat had sprung a plank forward and water was flooding into the hold. It would be a near thing, but the mate thought that as long as the pumps held, they would make Cleveland where he could slide her safely on a sandbar in the harbor.

The captain burst into the pilothouse and yelled something about the rudder quadrant loosening up, then dashed back out again into the storm. Alarmed at the captain's words, the mate followed. The decks were deserted, the crew either in the engine room desperately throwing cordwood into the boiler fire or below decks, out of the fury of the storm.

When the mate caught up with the captain, he was leaning over the stern rail and pointing at something below. The mate looked over the rail to see just as the captain staggered back several steps and pulled a big revolver out of his jacket pocket, pointing the business end at the mate's back. The mate saw nothing in the dark water and when he stood up and turned to tell the captain so, the revolver roared four times. The long sharp flame that shot out of the barrel punctuated the scene in eerie yellow flashes of light. Three of the big .44 caliber slugs tore deep into the mate's chest, driving him against the rail. The fourth went wide, burying itself in the wood rail. The mate thumped heavily to the deck as the torrents of rain washed the gushing blood into the scuppers and on into the lake. The captain threw the revolver into the water.

The horrified wife stepped hesitatingly out of the shadows and asked if he was dead. The captain assured her he was. From a corner, the captain pulled a 12-foot length of iron chain and wrapped it securely around the mate's body. The body had to stay down and not come floating ashore with the bullet holes telling a murderous tale. With the wife at the feet and captain at the torso, they hefted the mate up and rolled him over the rail into the lake. They didn't even hear the splash in the noise of the storm.

Together they made their way to the pilothouse where they found the engineer waiting. The red haired Scot said his steam pumps were failing and couldn't keep up with the water flooding into the hold. He figured they had an hour, perhaps, before the water doused his boiler fire. Then they would sink in minutes. The captain told him to get the crew together and prepare to launch the lifeboats. When the engineer said this was the mate's job and asked where he was, the captain replied he was just lost overboard. The engineer was shocked at the news, but said nothing and left to follow the captain's orders. The captain and wife went down to his cabin, where he broke open a bottle of whiskey and took a long gulp. He then passed it to the wife and sat on his bunk. Wordlessly she too took a deep swallow, coughing as the burning liquid ran down her throat.

From his cabin window the captain had a view out to the open Texas deck. Suddenly he jumped up and ran to the glass, looking outside into the storm. Anxiously he turned to the wife and asked if she had seen anything. She shook her head and took another swallow of the whiskey. As the captain turned away from the window, his door flew into splinters. When both captain and wife turned toward the crash they saw the dead mate standing framed in the doorway. Lightning rippled in the sky behind him. He was dripping wet and the chain was still wrapped around his waist. Three gaping holes were in his chest. More ominously, he held a fire axe firmly in his powerful hands.

The captain and wife froze with fear. The mate's axe cut quickly into the captain's chest, neatly cutting through muscle and bone to slice his heart in half. The captain fell to his knees, then pitched forward. The second swing cleaved the wife's head cleanly off, sending it spinning wildly to the deck. Blood spurted upward in a red fountain from her neck as the body did a half pirouette to the deck. Satisfied, the mate tossed the bloody axe down and staggered out of the cabin and into the raging storm.

When it looked like the ship was getting ready to plunge for the lake bottom, the engineer ordered one lifeboat away but kept the other back while he quickly searched for the missing captain and wife. When he entered the cabin and saw the bloody carnage, he was violently ill. Recovering, he ran back to the lifeboat, climbed in and had the men shove off. He told the crew neither captain or wife would be joining them, as both must have been washed overboard.

Neither lifeboat survived the storm. One was found smashed on the beach three days later. The other just disappeared. The bodies of perhaps half the crew were eventually located. The rest were just gone, kept by the lake forever.

The steamboat however did not sink. Waterlogged, it drifted for a full day until the storm abated, then grounded on a bar west of Long Point. When the lifesavers boarded the smashed and battered vessel the next day, they found no one until they reached the captain's cabin. There they discovered blood spattered everywhere. The captain lay in a heap against the bulwark and the wife spread eagled across the middle of the cabin. They found her head under the bed. Two empty whiskey bottles were next to it. A blood soaked axe was in the corner.

The searchers had all but concluded that no one was alive, when they found a wheelman still in the pilothouse, huddled fearfully behind a small chart table. When the engineer abandoned ship, he apparently forgot about him. All the while he was loyally at his post, waiting for orders that never came. Deep in shock, he gave no information on the double murder.

Since this was clearly a police matter, the keeper called in the law. When these worthies investigated, they could reach no conclusion other than it was obviously murder most foul. But by whom or why was unknown. Because of the brutal nature of the crime and the strange circumstances, it was hushed up very well. The police thought about charging the wheelman, but other than his surviving the wreck there was no evidence that he had any part in it. After all, if it were another crewmen who committed the terrible crime, he was dead anyway. What good would it do to drag the whole thing into the papers?

My great uncle was one of the investigating policemen. He was quite a smart guy and after the incident was officially closed, took the time to do his own investigating. He interviewed everyone connected with the boat and with a lot of conjecture, was able to piece together this tale from the different scraps of information he found.

He concluded that the wheelman was the key. He was the nearest thing to a witness. He may not have seen the actual crime, but he knew everyone involved and the overall circumstances. He had the key, although he probably didn't know it. My uncle only got him to talk 10 years later and then it was in a saloon with enough whiskey to loosen his tongue.

The man was in the pilothouse when the captain and mate ran out, not to return. He had heard the comment about the rudder and surmised that was where they were heading. Under the influence of the whiskey he also claimed to having seen the creature that was the mate climb up over the side of the ship, come up the companionway to just outside the pilothouse door and take a fire axe off the bulwark, then stagger back to the captain's cabin. When the wheelman saw the horrible look on his face, the chain around the waist, holes in the chest and dead staring eyes, he almost fainted dead away. Instead he ducked down and hid below the window framing. By now the boat was virtually powerless, so wheeling was useless anyway. After a minute or two he looked back toward the cabin in time to see the mate come out the door and jump back into the lake. He ducked back to his corner, where he remained until the lifesavers found him. Knowing no one would believe him, he said nothing about it.

There was some circumstantial evidence to support this wild story. During the original investigation, my great uncle carefully examined the stern rail and found the .44 caliber slug in the rail. At the time there was no explanation for it. An axe was also missing from the outside of the pilothouse. This was clearly the murder weapon found in the cabin. The wheelman later explained the rumors of the wife's infidelity and finding the bodies in the cabin with the whiskey only confirmed it. The mate certainly had motive for revenge against the captain for stealing his wife and, perhaps, based on the very circumstantial evidence, for his own death too. The wheelman's incredible description of the mate's bullet-riddled body coming out of the water was crazy, but then again strange things do happen on the lakes. There were obviously a number of big gaps and guesswork in the entire tale, but all that considered, it does explain the mystery. My great uncle always believed that the mate was the killer and that he either died in the storm or committed suicide afterward. But I always had the impression that he wasn't all that sure whether the mate did it before or after he was dead.

The owners turned the vessel over to the underwriters as a total loss. In the end, she was salvaged and rebuilt into a freighter. She sailed for another 10 years or so, but it was always as a haunted ship with a terrible reputation. During storms, the crew claimed that they sometimes saw a man with an axe walking the decks looking for something. An old cook claimed he once saw a headless woman on her hands and knees in the cabin aft of the Texas deck. She, too, appeared to be searching for something. The old wheelman would never set foot on her again and even avoided looking at the ship when she came into view.[69]

Spout

Some incidents defy all explanation. The October 10, 1997, issue of the *World Maritime News* reported that on October 4, 1997, while passing White Shoal Light en route to Charlevoix, the 552-foot steamer *Medusa Challenger* encountered a water spout. Instead of remaining harmlessly on the water, it leaped to the steamer's deck and lifted the heavy spotlight on the bridge wing out of its holder and elevated a bicycle on deck. The phenomenon lasted for a full 10 minutes.[70]

The Dead Cook

In the 1870s there was a story about a schooner lying in Port Colborne, Ontario, on Lake Ontario, because one of her last crew saw the ghost of a female cook floating over the vessel in a gale of wind. When the schooner reached Port Colborne, after being forced to run back by a storm, the sailors grabbed their bags and jumped ashore, wanting nothing to do with a haunted ship. The men claimed that two years before a woman cook had been killed when she was crushed between the vessel and another schooner. Ever since, her ghost haunted the ship.[71]

CHAPTER 8

Superstitions

Dreams

Sailors' dreams sometimes made news as evidenced by the following items from the *Marine Review.* "There died recently at East Jordan, Michigan, a man, the sunshine and shadows of whose life were intermingled with a peculiar fulfillment of superstitions, prophesy, the loss of his vessel in a collision and the death of his mother following a dream announcing the fact. His own death came after a deep sleep that had haunted him for years. All make up a peculiar and strange combination of related facts and superstitions.

"Captain James Ward was born in Nova Scotia 68 years ago. He left the land of his birth at the age of 17, after learning the hardships of sailing the perilous coast of his native land and secured work as a sailor before the mast on the lakes. He became well off, had a good home of the shore of Lake Erie at Port Burwell, Canada. He sailed for 40 years his own and other vessels and that presentiment could neither be coaxed nor shamed out of him.

"On the night of September 20, 1881, while going down the Detroit River in the schooner *Victor,* Captain Ward was in his berth asleep. He had a most distressing dream, that his mother was dying in far-away Nova Scotia and that his two brothers, then long dead, were standing at his bedside. He was so troubled by the visitation that he went on deck, only to see a big black boat directly ahead, which crashed into them. The *Victor* sank almost immediately and the captain, with his daughter and son, narrowly escaped drowning. It was a collision with the steam barge *S.J. Macy* just opposite Windsor.

"Captain Ward, upon going to the telegraph officer to announce to his family the news of the accident, found awaiting him a telegram announcing the death of his mother the night before. He quit sailing at once, sold out and went farming in Michigan, a discouraged man. He died after a lingering sickness of the most distressing sort, after lying in a deep sleep or trance for five or six days, just as he had predicted."[72]

A Canadian sailor, Henry McConnell, remembered a dream of wreck and rescue. In 1883 he was bound up Lake Erie on the topsail schooner *James R. Benson.* He was fast asleep in the forecastle, when another sailor, Tony Mallie, woke him, claiming he had heard the call and it was eight bells and time for their watch. When the pair tumbled on deck they were told they were two hours early! Muttering, they returned to the forecastle. Mallie apologized to McConnell, saying he must have dreamed that George the Greek, another member of the crew, had come down and woke him for the watch. Mallie also said that just before the dream, he had another, that the *Benson* "had rolled over with us and we were having a fearful time getting the cook on the side of the vessel."

Two hours later they were back on deck, but the weather had turned squally and the watch they were relieving was kept on deck to help shorten sail. The sky erupted and an unexpectedly powerful burst of wind knocked the schooner over on her beam ends. George the Greek, who was on the lee side halyards, immediately went under and was lost. The rest of the crew, except for the woman cook, managed to scamper up the side of the vessel, eventually riding safely on her upturned bottom. The cook had washed out the cabin door, ending up in the lake. She was the captain's wife, a great cook and a mother figure to the entire crew. She also weighed 200 pounds and it took a tremendous effort on the part of the crew to haul her back aboard. The survivors were later rescued after a passing schooner's sharp-eyed lookout spotted their hull awash in the cresting waves. Everything happened exactly as Tony Mallie dreamed it.[73]

The November 22, 1879, loss of the 135-foot, 465-ton Canadian side-wheeler *Waubuno* is a classic example of dream intervention. Even the name, an Algonquin word for "sorcerer," lends itself to thinking about "things beyond." Ominously, it was also the ship's second name, originally being launched in 1865 at Thorold, Ontario, on Lake Huron's Georgian Bay as the *Wawatam.*

The *Waubuno* was delayed in Collingwood en route for Parry Sound, waiting out a northwest gale. Rather than stay aboard the cramped steamer, many passengers elected to sleep in a more comfortable local hotel. Two of the passengers were a Dr. W.H. Doupe and his young bride, both from Mitchell, Ontario. The trip on the *Waubuno* was to be part of their honeymoon. They were heading for the small town of McKellar, near Parry Sound where he would open his practice.

That night, Mrs. Doupe had a terrifying dream. She recalled a "great weight pressing them (passengers) down." In her dream she saw the crew and passengers swallowed by the cold, dark lake. When the storm eventually lessened, and the captain blew his whistle at 4 a.m. to call the passengers back to the boat, she implored her husband for them not to board the steamer but to stay safe ashore. Other passengers heard her protests and explanation of the eerie dream. Some took heed and stayed behind. Others ignored the ranting of a "hysterical" woman.

The *Waubuno* steamed out of Collingwood and into legend. What actually happened will never be known but the steamer perished with all 24 souls aboard. The last man to see her in this world was the Christian Island lightkeeper, as she passed two miles offshore. The storm had increased in ferocity and the small steamer must have struggled mightily. Some hours later, lumberjacks near Moon River heard what they thought was the *Waubuno*'s whistle, but paid it no special attention. When she didn't arrive at Parry Sound, a quick search was made.

Her paddlebox with the name printed on it was found as was part of the Doupe's furniture and a single empty lifeboat. Every little island was combed in the desperate hope that at least one survivor had made it ashore. There were none. The men also found or accounted for every lifebelt carried by the steamer. Not one was ever used. Whatever happened was so quick, there was no time for an action as simple as putting on a lifebelt.

The following spring, an Ojibway hunter discovered the hull upside down in a lonely bay near Moose Point. Marine men surmised that she rolled in heavy seas during the night of the gale. Obviously, on things less tangible than dreams do our lives hang. If Dr. Doupe had only listened to his wife.[74]

There may well be a ghost associated with the *Waubuno*. In the late 1980s, a pleasure boater stopped at Wreck Island for a swim and felt a strong presence of someone or something watching him. The island was named for its proximity to the disaster. He also briefly sighted the fleeting image of what he thought was a woman dressed in dark colored, full length dress. Was it the wandering spirit of Mrs. Doupe or another of the *Waubuno*'s lost souls?

A woman's dream foretold the end of the old Waubuno. *K.E. THRO COLLECTION*

It's been said that misfortune comes in threes and so it proved for the owners of the *Waubuno,* the Georgian Bay Navigation Company. First it was the *Waubuno* in November of 1879. Then the 162-foot *Manitoulin,* purchased to replace the *Waubuno,* burned with loss of life on May 19, 1882. Finally the 136-foot *Asia,* chartered from the Northwestern Transportation Company, sank in Georgian Bay on September 14, 1882, with an estimated 123 lives lost. The board of directors were hard-pressed to explain the unnatural trio of disasters.[75]

Twenty-seven years to the day after the *Waubuno* perished, another vessel disappeared under a similar cloud of mystery. The small steamer *J.H. Jones* left her Owen Sound dock and sailed into a storm and complete oblivion. Not a body of her passengers or crew was ever found. Only scattered wreckage along the shore testified to her end.[76]

Launchings

Old sailors believed the most critical event in any vessel's life is its launching. If it went well, the ship would have a long and prosperous career. However, if the launching went wrong, the ship would be forever cursed. Sailors, owners and shipyards went to great effort to assure that the launching went smoothly. A vessel that "stuck" or hesitated on its slide down the inclined launching ways meant that she would have an ill-starred career. When the tug *Maytham* was launched the *Buffalo Express* commented, "Everything went off smoothly, including the boat without accident, thus foreshadowing good fortune to the craft in the future."[77]

157

An example of a vessel that refused to leave her ways was the steamer *Saginaw Valley.* The first attempt to launch was on June 2, 1888, but when the blocks were knocked free she refused to budge. Her builders tried twice more that day, but without success. In preparation for the fourth try on June 20, the steamer was jacked up to give it more slope to run, but still she only came down four feet. Even with the tugs *Wilson* and *Byers* pulling, only four more feet were gained. Old sailors viewed the entire incident with great apprehension.[78]

When the schooner *Bay Queen* was built in 1857 in Dover, Ontario, she was fully rigged before launching. Despite supposedly being ready for the lake, when the big day came she stubbornly refused to budge. The superstitious predicted an ill-starred career. It may have been ill-starred, but nevertheless it was long. Later rebuilt as the *Dauntless,* after apparently wrecking near Port Colborne in 1866, she finally sank in Lake Ontario in 1894.[79]

The 245-foot *Minnedosa,* the largest Canadian schooner ever built on the lakes, was another example of a vessel with an ill-starred launching yet long career. When she was supposed to launch at her Kingston shipyard on April 20, 1890, she remained fast. The big schooner stayed glued to her ways. All the soap in the county made no difference. The tremendous weight of the vessel had broken and spread her underwater slide ways. It took difficult and dangerous work by a hard hat diver to clear the damage and two powerful tugs to start her moving before she finally took to the water. The *Minnedosa's* career ended on October 20, 1905, when she was caught in a gale off Harbor Beach, Michigan, Lake Huron. Deeply laden with 75,000 bushels of wheat, she dove for the bottom taking six men with her.[80]

Some vessels take the occasion of their launching to make a point about their independence. An example was the USS *Michigan,* the first iron ship built for the U.S. Navy. In December 1843, she stood ready to be launched into Lake Erie. Try as they might and to their great embarrassment, the yard crew could not get her to budge. The crowd that had gathered to witness this historic moment grew more and more impatient, but the *Michigan* refused to cooperate. Hammers, blocks, wedges, colorful statements of parentage and outright threats failed to move her. Reluctantly, everyone gave up and went home. When the shipyard crew returned the next day, they discovered to their great surprise, that the warship was floating, patiently waiting for them. She had just apparently launched herself during a furious night windstorm. Did the ship's spirit just take over?[81]

The *Michigan* was also famous for her "wishing chair" owned by the captain's steward. The mysterious chair was given to him in Amherstburg, Ontario, when the vessel made a short visit there in 1890. Legend claims that anyone who sat in the chair and made a wish was certain to have it granted. There were many testimonials to its effectiveness.[82]

When the big steel steamer *John McGean* was lost in the great November 1913 storm, many old timers remembered that when she launched in Lorain, Ohio, on February 22, 1908, she experienced problems. When she hit the water, the resulting wave washed into a crowd of spectators, sweeping many into the water. At least two sustained injuries. Such a bad launching foretold a bad career and, at least in the case of the *McGean,* it was true.[83]

Saint Elmo's Fire and the Northern Lights

Saint Elmo's Fire, also known under the terms corpse light, corposants, Jacob's lantern or Jack-o'-lantern, is often viewed as a bad omen. Some men fresh from the Atlantic coast thought it was the spirits of drowned men climbing back aboard to ask for prayers for their salvation. Old whalermen believed that it was the soul of a sailor who died aboard.

On Lake Huron it is most common just before or just after a storm. On Lake Erie it is said to appear in muggy weather just before or after an electrical storm. It gives a dull glow around the top of masts and end of the spar. Some believe that it means death to anyone who looks on it. Others think it brings good luck to the first man who sees it.

Some think that St. Elmo's Fire is a good omen as indicated by this short poem.

Safe comes the ship to harbor,
Through billows and through gales,
If the great twin brethren,
Set shining on her sails.[84]

In another instance, on a very dark and foggy night on Lake Ontario, the St. Elmo's Fire was so bright that it allowed the crew to see the rigging by its eerie glow. It was not considered an ill omen.[85]

Some sailors thought that if it was seen to rise, it was a favorable sign. If it descended, the opposite was true. Shining directly into a sailor's face was considered bad luck as was the fire on a rudder.

One Lake Erie skipper, however, was so afraid of St. Elmo's Fire that during an August 1893 storm when the wheelman pointed out some on the steering pole, he immediately ordered a change of course to the nearest land, which was the port of Erie, Pennsylvania. All the way in the vessel rolled badly in the wave trough and only after considerable struggle safely made the harbor. The boat was so beat up it took the crew three days to stow the freight. While laying safe in Erie, a storm lashed the lake, sinking the big steamer *Dean Richmond* with all hands as well as four other vessels. The captain believed that by running to port at the St. Elmo's Fire warning, he had escaped the same fate.[86]

In the fall of 1872, while the schooner *Magdala* was booming across Lake Ontario in squally weather, the crew was treated to a rare display of corpse light. The night was black as sin with the men literally unable to see their hands in front of their faces. Without warning, the deck was illuminated by an eerie light from above. It's source was initially the fly high up on the topmast truck.

The fly was a cone of light canvas three to four yards long tapered to a point and kept open by a foot-wide wooden hoop. While a brightly colored fly added a certain smartness to a vessel, the real purpose was as a "tell-tale" or wind sock.

Down from the eyes of the fly "blazed a cold white lamp as big as a floodlight." Also, "… at regular intervals, all the way down the topmast rigging of both masts, from the eyes to the crosstrees and on the topmast stays and triadic stay and out on the ends of the crosstree legs, balls of pale cold light burned. Not in flashes, but in a steady glow, moving from place to place, but seemingly favoring points, such as the topmast trucks and crosstree ends." Since the eerie light helped the crew as they fought to stow a flapping foresail, they thought it a good omen.[87]

Some mariners consider the northern lights to be a good sign, others a bad one. Beaver Islanders on Lake Michigan believed that a bad storm would follow within three days after a display of the colorful aurora.[88] Men of Scandinavian stock remembered the tales of their forefathers claiming that the flashing lights were the reflection of the brilliant armor of the Valkyries as they rode the heavens searching for fallen warriors.

The Three Sisters

A traditional belief on the lakes, especially on Lake Superior, concerns the infamous three sisters, sailor lore to describe a vessel being struck by three huge waves in rapid succession. The first two waves come close together. The third runs a bit behind, but is far bigger than the first two. It's the third wave that dooms the ship.

Old time sailors attribute many losses to the three sisters. Some mariners believe it was the three sisters that sank the *Edmund Fitzgerald*.

A variation of the phenomenon has the first wave washing water on the deck, quickly followed by the second wave. The third, a larger wave, puts enough water aboard to doom the ship.

When the three sisters were growling bad, captains knew they had to be especially careful in trying a turn. Timing was everything. If they made a mistake, the ship could get caught in the deadly wave trough and all would be lost. They had to watch carefully for their chance and when it came, take it without hesitation.[89]

Corpses Aboard

Having a corpse aboard was always considered bad luck. Sometimes however it became the instrument of black humor. In one instance a vessel took a corpse-filled coffin aboard at Harbor Beach, Michigan, bound for a Lake Erie port.

The crew, of course, was not happy with the cargo. A crewman, seeing the opportunity for a good joke, waited until the ship was well under way and then hid behind the box and began tapping on it. In a low voice he said, "Let me out, let me out." The rest of the crew was ready to jump overboard with fear, before the trick was revealed.[90]

A more serious incident occurred on September 29, 1872, on the Canadian steamer *Lake Michigan* bound for Chicago. The crew's apprehension started when a Canadian family boarded with a very ominous bit of freight, the exhumed casket of a relative who had died 27 years before. The family was relocating to Illinois and felt it necessary to bring "all" the family along.

Downbound on Lake Michigan, a terrific gale smashed into her. Battered by the stress of the weather, the engine failed and the steamer was left to the tender mercy of the crashing seas. As the storm increased in force, the crew became more and more concerned, "knowing" the supernatural aspects of their putrefying cargo.

To save themselves, the crew threw the corpse-filled casket they were carrying overboard. The tempest soon abated and the steamer *Lac La Belle* appeared on the scene to rescue the sailors. Eventually, a tug towed the disabled steamer to safety.

The crew was absolutely convinced that their action of dumping the coffin ridded them of its curse and therefore saved their lives![91]

The "lucky" mate of the steamer **Wexford** missed the boat before she went missing in the great storm of 1913. AUTHOR'S COLLECTION

A Lucky Jonah?

The storm that ravaged the Great Lakes in November 1913 was a terrible one. When the winds and seas finally calmed, an estimated 244 sailors were drowned and 17 vessels completely wrecked. Among the lost vessels was the steel steamer *Wexford* that disappeared in Lake Ontario with all 17 hands.

The first mate of the *Wexford* was one James McCutcheon. As fate would have it, he missed the boat when she departed Sarnia, thus he later became a key witness in identifying the bodies of his old shipmates as they came ashore. The *Wexford* was the *third* boat he had missed in his career and each had wrecked! Was he lucky – or some kind of Jonah?

The Friday Curse

The Friday curse dies hard. Many still believe it is bad luck to start the season on a Friday. For example, the *Walter J. McCarthy*, a 1,000-footer owned by the American Steamship Company, was prepared to start the 1998 season at 8 p.m. on Friday, March 13. She had just finished loading coal at the Superior Energy Dock in Superior, Wisconsin, and was ready to sail for Taconite Harbor, Minnesota. Instead she delayed until 12.01 Saturday. There was no reason to tempt fate with a double hex of a Friday and a 13!

The Canadian tug *Fred A. Lee* was a vessel that flaunted superstition. It was launched on a 13th, lost on a Friday the 13th and sank 13 miles off Point aux Barques, Lake Huron.

The 70-foot tug slid down the ways on June 13, 1896. While at least it wasn't a Friday the 13th – but a Saturday – doubtless many old-timers considered it a mistake to conduct such an important ceremony on the 13th. Why take chances? Despite their fears, her working career was relatively long and uneventful, certainly at odds with such an unlucky beginning. But in the end, the 13th curse struck anyway.

The *Lee* left Sarnia, Ontario, during the morning of November 12, 1936, bound for winter quarters at Sault Ste. Marie, Ontario. She had spent the season working for the Wallaceburg Sand and Gravel Company of Wallaceburg, Ontario. The job was done and the five-man crew was anxious to get home.

During the night of the 12th the tug managed to stray off course and slid aground near Harbor Beach, Michigan, about 60 miles north of Sarnia. The Harbor Beach Coast Guard pulled her free and the *Lee* continued on for the Sault.

The story is next picked up by the crew of the freighter *John G. Munson*. About 4 p.m. on November 13, she was coming southward around Point aux Barques and her mate was watching the tug coming north, about two miles distant. There were no other ships visible, so the tug drew his full attention. He looked away for a minute, then glanced back. The tug was gone! Grabbing his binoculars he searched for it but found only empty lake. The captain swung the ship toward where the tug had been and a quarter of an hour later they passed through a small wreckage field. There wasn't much left. A small amount of wood from the pilothouse, a mattress, wood chair and some pillows were all they found. There were neither survivors nor bodies.

The best theory of the cause of the disaster was a boiler explosion. It could have been caused by a leak started when she went aground, the water rising unnoticed until it hit the hot boilers. The explosion also could have been caused by mud pumped in while aground, plugging some boiler tubes, then letting go while under way, sending a shot of cold water into the hot boiler that resulted in an explosion.

But when all was said and done, the tug was launched on a 13th and sunk 13 miles off Point aux Barques on a Friday the 13th. Was it all coincidence or something else?

Cats

While rats were welcome aboard, cats never were. The old sailors thought that they only brought bad luck, as evidenced by this October 30, 1857, *Detroit Free Press* article.

"A Canadian vessel arrived in port a few days since, the captain of which is a genuine John Bull. Being accosted by a brother sailor, who inquired as to the kind of weather he experienced on the trip, he replied, 'Vy, it blowed and it stormed and snowed and pelted like hold 'arry for 'af a week steady, and the hold vessel's timbers began to creak like a rickety door – there seemed to be no hend to the gale, when all at once I hespied a cat on board; so without stopping a moment to think, I 'bout ship and put for the Manitous, where I landed the cat safe 'igh and dry. From that moment the wind fell and we got hinto port without a contrary breath of wind.'

"We call the attention of lake captains and underwriters to this important discovery. They ought to see that no Jonahs, in the shape of poor puss, get aboard before they start out from port in these squally times. – *Chicago Press*"[92]

Rats

A ship didn't need a full career as a hoodoo for sailors to know when the end was coming near. A case in point is the schooner *Amaranth*. The 134-foot schooner, built in Milan, Ohio, in 1864, was at the end of a long career when she hit her final storm on Lake Huron in September 1901.

She was in tow of the steamer *John H. Pauley* when the northeast gale rolled into her. It was too strong for the steamer to keep either the barge or herself off the beach and both vessels went ashore. The *Amaranth* broached as she was going in and quickly broke up in the waves. The steamer had removed her crew just before she went over, thus certainly saving their lives.

Later, some of the rescued men claimed they knew the schooner was doomed before they left port. One said he had watched rats running ashore on her lines as they were loading their lumber cargo. The captain stated that while in port a canary landed on his shoulder, another sure sign of impending disaster![93]

Mirages

Mirages were also seen as harbingers of doom and disaster. The mirages were caused by the difference in temperature between the air and water and were most notable in the summer. Mountains and cliffs projected from where there were none and islands rose up from mid-lake. After a while all would disappear, melting into sky and water. Often objects appeared inverted. Sometimes when the mirage was of a vessel, it may have been referred to as a ghost ship, but it was always considered a sign of bad luck.

Once on Lake Superior a schooner crew saw a "ghost ship" sailing along at a distance "in sections." The crew was certain dire things would happen. Later, the ship was seen to come together and then appear very natural before it vanished.

When the crew of a schooner out of Marquette, Michigan, on Lake Superior, sighted the mirage of a schooner high over the horizon, they were certain disaster was soon to happen. When they reached the Soo they told the captain they wanted to get off, but he wouldn't let them. There is no record of what happened to the schooner, whether it succumbed to accident or arrived safely.

The range of mirages could be extraordinary. In one instance a schooner was bound for Ashland, Wisconsin, Lake Superior, for iron ore when the crew sighted Outer Island Light 70 miles out. After briefly losing it, they soon picked it up again. Although all aboard became very worried, nothing weird occurred. Such mirages were also common on Lake Michigan. The crew of a schooner 100 miles from Chicago clearly saw the city waterfront above the horizon. The crews of the Lake Michigan car ferries often saw mirages and many feared them.[94]

Just at sunset on a day in August 1856, the steamer *Bay State* on Lake Ontario reported seeing a mirage consisting of a dozen sailing vessels inverted. At the time the sky was overcast and a thick haze blanketed the lake. The visible details of the vessels were remarkable. The outline of the rigging and sails were clearly seen. The phenomenon continued until dark.[95]

The *Oswego Palladium* of June 10, 1873, reported a truly rare sight. "Captain Estes, a gentlemen known for many years in command of Lake Ontario steamers, informs us that he was the witness a few nights since of a wonderful phenomenon on Lake Ontario, the like of which he never saw before and does not expect to see again. While on his way from the St. Lawrence up the lake on the steam tug of which he is the master and when near the islands known as the False Ducks, and while standing at the wheel, there suddenly burst in view the city of Oswego – 31 miles distant – with the gaslight in the streets and all the appearances that a town lighted up would present from a hill in the immediate vicinity at night. The lighthouse at Oswego, as well as a dozen others on the lake shore below as far as Sackets Harbor, were distinctly seen. It was sort of a night mirage. This display was witnessed for several minutes then slowly faded away into darkness. Such wonderful spectacles are rarely seen either on land or water."[96]

In June 1887, Captain Leith and the crew of the schooner *Lizzie A. Law* saw another remarkable mirage. While on Lake

Michigan and abreast of Cana Island, Wisconsin, a pall of mist cleared and they saw the Manitou Islands rising sharp on the horizon. At the time the islands were still 40 miles to the east! The mirage was keen enough that the "beach, the forests and even the lighthouse could be plainly seen without the aid of a glass."[97]

Chapter 9

Sea Serpents

Sea Serpents

The lakes continue to be the home of various forms of sea serpents and other monsters of the deep as evidenced by period newspapers. Some were clearly "tongue in cheek," while others were of a more serious tone.

Oswego Palladium, Friday, Sept. 14, 1821

"From the *Niagara Democrat* – It will be seen by the following depositions that the western lakes are like to engender as big snakes as the Atlantic, though the inhabitants on their margin have hitherto been prolific in the manufacture of big stories to correspond – an advantage long enjoyed by our Yankee Atlantic brethren.

"The Sea Serpent Navigating The Western Lakes.

"Mr. Editor, Sir – The following affidavits of John Maupin of Montreal, and James Sigler of Jefferson Co., N.Y., describe a very large and singular animal that has made its appearance in Lake Ontario, resembling that celebrated sea fish or snake, which has crowded the columns of the eastern papers for the last two or three summers. This, there is but little doubt, is one of the same species, and that which was seen ascending the St. Lawrence last spring by some boatmen. W.H. personally appeared before me, G.S. Keefer, Esquire, one of his majesty's Justices of the Peace in and for the District of Niagara, John Maupin and James Sigler, and deposeth as follows:

– That on the morning of the 25th July, 1821, about 100 miles from Niagara and about 20 from land, aboard the canoe *Light-foot,* on our passage from Montreal to Mackinac, in company with eight voyageurs, we discovered at the distance of five or six hundred yards a large body floating on the surface of the water, very much like a burnt log from 20 to 25 feet length; but on approaching it three or four hundred yards closer, it proved to be an animal motionless and apparently asleep. We continued to advance towards it until within 30 yards, when the animal raised its head about 10 feet out of the water, looking around him in the most awful and ferocious manner, and darting forward with great velocity, making the water fly in every direction, and throwing columns of it at a vertical height of seven or eight feet with his tail.

"After having gone in a western direction about one or two miles, he appeared to resume his former state, we then resolved to attack him, and accordingly loaded our guns for this purpose, and moved slowly toward him within gunshot. We here had a good view of the animal, he is at least 37 feet long, $2^{1}/_{2}$ feet in diameter (if measured through the thickest part of the body), is covered with black scales which appeared to create consternation only, he disappearing as before – he has a tremendous head and similar to that of a common snake – frequently thrusting from his mouth a large red and venomous looking tongue. After the animal disappeared we continued our course with a lively oar as may well be imagined. His figure when in motion is serpentine. – Sworn to, signed, &C. In due form.

"The editors of the *Boston Gazette* offer a reward of $10,000 for the Sea Serpent, dead or alive. His snakeship was seen at Nahant; his head was raised about 13 feet out of water, and is shaped like that of a horse; he is about the thickness of a barrel and is 60 feet long."

Oswego Palladium, July 1, 1833
"The American Sea Serpent in Lake Ontario. – Our office has been favored with a visit from Captain Abijah Kellogg of the schooner *Polythermus,* of Sacket's arrived this morning from Rochester. This gentleman has related to us such a tale of wonder, a tale so incredible, that we scruple some, as the Yankees say it, laying his narration before our readers, lest they might think it but the creation of your imagination. Capt. Kellogg states: – yesterday evening (June 15th) about 7 o'clock, as he was making for Kingston harbor, the 'Ducks' bearing N. by W. distant two miles, he saw something lying still on the weather bow that looked like the mast of a vessel. Observing it more attentively, he was surprised and alarmed to see it in motion, and steering towards the schooner. –

Singing out to his hands to take care of themselves, he put the schooner up to the wind, lashed the helm a lee, and run up the main rigging, waiting for the monster to approach. The serpent, for it was no other than an immense snake, neared the vessel fast and passed immediately under her stern, taking no notice whatever of the schooner or those on board, but affording to everybody an ample opportunity to observe and note his monstrous dimensions. In length he was about 175 feet, of a dark blue color, spotted with brown; towards either end he tapered off, but about the middle his body was of the circumference of a flour barrel, his head was peculiarly small and could not well be distinguished but from the direction in which he moved. He swam with an undulating movement, keeping the best part of his body under water, but occasionally showing his entire length. He was in sight full 15 minutes and when last seen was making the best of his way down the St. Lawrence. On board the schooner were two young men, the vessel's crew, together with three passengers, who are willing to be qualified to the truth of what has been here stated (*British Whig*)."[98]

An Old Tar's Twister

"In the summer of '40, I think it was, a schooner I was in cut a sea sarpint in two. We stood out from Kingston about noon with the wind from the nor'east, a pipin' rather strong, and as the schooner was flyin' light, she traveled astonishin' to see. Just after passin' the Ducks the 'old man,' who was pacin' the deck, called the mate's attention to sumthin' in the water about a quarter of a mile dead ahead. Lookin' off that way a long object, resemblin' the back of a shoal, was plainly seen. For a minute or two the 'old man' was in doubt what to do, but finally concludin' that a shoal had no business in such a place, he ordered the man at the wheel to steer dead for it.

"All of us on deck, exceptin' the man at the wheel, run for'ard to get a sight of the obstruction and got on the forecastle deck jest in time to see that the thing was nothin' more nor less than a huge sea sarpint, sound asleep. The monster wasn't less'n 50 feet long, with a head sumthin' similar to that of the fiery dragon we see in picter books. It was a full dull brown color, scales on its back, hair jest back of the neck, and a tail like a harpoon head. In less time than it takes to tell it we was atop the monster and crushin' its bones in an awful way.

"Our headway was deadened a trifle but we kept on, and as the monster come up under our stern we could see we had cut it clean in two and the two halves was swimmin' away in opposite directions. Before then there hadn't been but one sea sarpint on Lake Ontario, but since then two have been seen most every year. Morton's distillery, near Kingston, was in full blast at that time, and I account for the sarpint bein' asleep this side of the Ducks instead of the other side of Snake Island, its usual haunt, by the fact that that mornin' the men at the distillery dumped two or three hundred bushels of mash into the lake and the sarpint had got a trifle 'how come you so.'

"Diamond of Napanee, who made quite a stir a few years ago by safely pilotin' the lost *Ivanhoe* from the Ducks into the upper gap of the Bay of Quinte, had a big tank built two or three years ago for the sarpint. The idea was to ketch the chap, put him into the tank and sell the whole thing to Barnum. The tank had a gate like a lock gate, and it was sunk in South Bay, the favorite feedin' place for the sarpint. The plan was to drive him into the tank, when the suction would close the gate and the wonder of the lakes would be trapped.

"The steam barges *Adventure* of Kingston, *Ivanhoe* of Napanee, and *Norman* of Belleville were to frighten the brute into the trap, and either one of them boats was fully able to the task. As luck would have it, the day the three boats left here there was a fog so thick the captains lost their reckonin' and when it cleared up the *Ivanhoe* was tryin' to get into Sandy Creek, the *Adventure* was up near Charlotte, and the *Norman* had turned completely 'round and was in the river runnin' a race with the plaster mill. The tank is still in the same spot and will stay there till Calvin & Breck launch their ship from Garden Island, hopin' that when she slides into the water the sarpint will rush into the tank in its anxiety to escape the huger monster.

"If the plan works, 'there's millions in it,' and the Bay grangers can keep their barley and handle it themselves or all turn maltsters and brewers."

Apparently, the capture scheme didn't work, because to this day it is claimed a sea serpent affectionately known as "Kingstie" still lurks in the waters around Kingston, Ontario.

Poking Fun

After a rash of sea serpent sightings in 1867 in Lake Ontario, the Pultneyville (New York) *Commercial Press* had enough of a sense of humor to print the following:

"The Sea Serpent. As the story has gone the rounds of the press that a sea serpent has been seen in our lake by parties at different times, it would perhaps be well to state for the benefit of the public, the facts in the case as they have been told to us. Mr. Henry Stowell, of Oswego, says he owns the animal of which so much has been said, having imported him at great expense from the Humbug Islands. He keeps him at Blind Sodus, at which place he has him boarded during the hot weather and, as soon as the weather becomes cool, he intends to skin him and have it stuffed, of which men are coming from New Bedford for that purpose. He sends him from Oswego two old canal horses a week, of which costs him but a trifle, and they are towed up behind the American Steamers, are cut adrift in the lake when opposite that place, when they are then towed in by boats for his use. It has been the intention of Mr. Stowell to keep him under close confinement, and for this purpose only was Blind Sodus selected for his home. He has occasionally stolen away and visited different localities about the lake, and when he has been seen, has made hideous noises in imitation of the parties present. Mr. S., has now sent up a horse tamer to subdue him."[99]

The Lake Monster

Detroit Free Press, August 9, 1867
"Description of the Animal By a Fisherman
"Communication of a Vessel Captain – The Monster Seen at Michigan City
"The *Chicago Tribune* says:
"That Lake Michigan is inhabited by a vast monster, part fish and part serpent, no longer admits of doubt. We have already published the fact that the crews of the tug *George W. Wood* and the propeller *Sky Lark* had seen him off Evanston, lashing the waves into a tempest. It is to be regretted that those vessels were not able to approach nearer to him, as from the (culled?) testimony of so many persons we might have been able to obtain an accurate idea of the nondescript. As it is, the evidence of the crews sufficiently establishes the fact that the animal is between 40 and 50 feet in length, his shape serpentine, the size of is neck about that of a human being and the size of his body about that of an ordinary barrel.
"The monster was not again seen until yesterday morning, when he suddenly made his appearance just below Hyde Park, about a mile and a half from shore, where the bed of the lake suddenly dips to a great depth. The facts that we are about to state we have derived from a fisherman living in that vicinity named Joseph Muhlke. Mr. Muhlke is an intelligent German who gains his living by fishing, and is well known to the residents of the southern

part of the city, where his cart and fish-box have been constant callers for the past three or four years. We have no reason to doubt his statement, as he is entirely honest, and had no means of knowing that others had seen the fish or described him. While their general statement is confirmed by him, he adds many details which are new.

"Mr. Muhlke, as is his custom, took boat and lines at daybreak yesterday morning, nearly to the edge of the flats, where fish are abundant, threw out his anchor and set his lines. It was a bright, clear morning, a gentle south breeze just rippling the surface of the lake, but not sufficiently strong to impart any motion to the boat. For some reason, his usual good fortune did not attend him. He fished on for about half an hour, and still no bites. It was now growing light very fast, and he determined to go in nearer to shore and fish awhile for perch, and return to his grounds after the sun was up. He therefore drew in his lines, and was about to weigh anchor, when he became aware of a singular motion of his boat. The ripple of the lake was not sufficient to cause it. There could not be a swell on the lake, as the weather had been very still during the past two or three days. Again the wind was from the south, and his boat was headed to the north, so that if the disturbance had been the result of natural causes his boat would naturally have had a corresponding motion, while in reality the motion was lateral, or from east to west, and different from that caused by a swell, not being long and gradual, but abrupt and broken. He turned his eyes to the eastward, but could see nothing, and still the motion of the boat increased. Alarmed by this unusual phenomenon, he again commenced pulling in his anchor, but was this time interrupted by a sound to the eastward – a peculiar noise, half puffing like a heavy breath and half an actual vocal sound, harsh and grating as the fisherman described it, like the noise a catfish makes when first caught, only a great deal louder and more frightful. He immediately let go of the rope and turned his eyes in the direction of the sound, and for the first time became aware of a dark object in the water, oval in shape, resembling very much a boat keel upward, and only about 80 rods distant [80 rods = about ¹/₄ mile or 400 meters].

"At first, the object seemed stationary, but as he watched it, it gradually increased in bulk, still preserving an oval, or rather the segment of a circle in form. Suddenly the motion ceased, the object apparently rising out of the water, at its highest point, about three or four feet. In a very short time, another object commenced rising about 20 feet nearer to him, as he judged, which he could clearly enough see was the head of some animal, as the eyes were plainly visible. Almost at the same time, the tail became apparent, equidistant from the first part of the animal he had seen. As he judged, about two-thirds of the monster was out of the water. Thus far the animal had made no forward motion, and manifested no disposition to do so, the only signs of activity displayed being a gentle motion of the head, north and south, as an occasional uplifting or stretching of a long neck out of the lake, and a few splashes of the tail upon the water, but not by any means with that fury described by the crews of the *Wood* and *Sky Lark*. The fisherman, rightly judging that an animal so huge would not approach the flats, determined to watch him until he could get a good idea of his general appearance.

"As we have said, his estimate of the length, which, he informs us, was five times the length of his boat, very nearly tallies with the previous accounts, while his estimate of the circumference is equally confirmatory. The general color of the animal was a bluish black, darkest in the center, graduating nearly to blue towards the head and tail. The underside of the animal was only visible as he lifted his head and tail occasionally, and this appeared to be of a grayish white, resembling the color of the dog-fish somewhat. The head was a little larger than the human average head, growing smaller toward the mouth, and sloping gradually toward the neck, somewhat like a seal's. Toward the snout, which was triangular in shape, the head was very much depressed, and on the extreme end of the snout, Mr. Muhlke thinks there were barbels, but of this he is not sure. No teeth were visible. The eyes were large, larger than the human eye, but of their color or shape, Mr. M. could form no idea whatever. Only a portion of the neck was visible. This appeared to be rough and along its upper surface and extending nearly to its tail, was a series of what looked like the bony plates of a sturgeon. This ridge extended over the first section of the animal, which, Mr. M. saw, but apart from this there was no appendage visible on the forward part of the animal. Mr. M., however, was confident that there were either fins or legs, toward the head and under the water, as there was a constant wash of the water on either side of him, near that point, as if he was sustaining his huge bulk by the motion of such appendages. A few feet forward of the tail there was a well developed fin of a greenish hue, corresponding with the dorsal fin of the sturgeon, but many times larger, and evidently more powerful. The entire fin had a lateral motion, and the various spines of which it was composed had an individual longitudinal motion, so that sometimes the fin almost closed up like a fan. Immediately beneath this was an anal fin, possessing the same characteristics, but different in shape, being very long and the spines of equal length. Immediately in front of this were two well developed legs. Mr. M. thinks they ended in a web foot. In any event, they were jointless, but were so flexible that the animal could draw them up to the belly when they were not in use. By analogy, therefore, we should infer that the animal had similar legs at his other extremity, which favors the supposition that he walks at times on the bed of the lake, in search of his prey, and at once banishes the supposition that he might be of the sturgeon family. The tail itself was of great size and strength, very unsymmetrical in shape, with something resembling long hair covering its entire upper surface, the under surface being diversified with sharp ridges, radiating to the outer edge."[100]

Nessie of the Straits

There are also reports of strange lake creatures being seen today. A St. Ignace, Michigan, husband and wife were standing on the Lake Huron shore in St. Ignace on Easter Sunday 1989. It was mid-morning and the weather was warm and pleasant. There was every indication of an early spring. The lake was calm with hardly a ripple to break the surface. While the wife was looking elsewhere, the husband noticed a "... large wake in the water heading northeast," toward Rabbit's Back Point. Quickly he pointed out the strange phenomenon to his wife. There was no boat or other obvious explanation for the wake. They returned swiftly to their home, about a mile and half distant, where there was a pair of powerful binoculars. Looking through the binoculars, the wife saw that the wake was not caused by a boat or jet ski. Instead, it was left by an object projecting about two feet out of the water, almost like a submarine's periscope. But why would a submarine be running between Mackinac Island and St. Ignace? After a while the strange wake disappeared behind Mackinaw Island. The couple were longtime residents of the area and had never seen anything like it before. This was not the first report of a "sea serpent" in the area. In August 1975, there was an account of a "40-foot snake-like creature" being sighted in the Straits, northbound from Cheboygan, Michigan.[101]

The Editor's Last Word

Perhaps the best interpretation of the early Great Lakes sea serpent stories was that of the *Detroit Democratic Free Press* of May 13, 1835.

"The Lake Serpent – Who has not heard of the enormous serpent or snake of Lake Superior? – If we mistake not, this frightful monster has been occasionally mentioned by different writers and travelers as inhabiting those mighty waters; nor can we imagine what should now have induced his departure therefrom. But to the facts.

"Yesterday between the hours of 5 p.m. and 6 p.m., a regular built snake, destitute of all appearance of a mane, and of those phrenological bumps or bunches which are said to be appurtenant to the old sea serpent – of slim formation, and apparently not less than 75 feet in length, and in the middle about 5 feet in circumference, or 20 inches in diameter – floating down the Detroit River, and passing the city, generally with his head elevated 5 to 8 feet, as in an attitude of surveying, alternately, the scenery presented on either shore – sometimes carried along by the current, coiled as if prepared to spring upon his prey, and at other times stretching forward, at full length, as if to exhibit himself for the gratification and astonishment of his beholders – his back of a dark brown color, his sides a deep green, and his belly a dingy white, without fins, with small green but glistening eyes, encircled with red – at last plunging forward as in sport, and disappearing in the depths of the majestic river – was not seen."

Then again it must be remembered that the editor never had the pleasure of seeing one either, only ridiculing those who did![102]

Glossary

Ballast
Bulk material carried for weight to stabilize ships, usually water.

Bark (Barque)
Sailing ship with three masts, two of which are square-rigged. On the Great Lakes the term is applied to BARKENTINES.

Barkentine
Sailing ship with three masts, the FOREmost of which is square-rigged. On the Great Lakes usually called BARKS.

Bilge
In general, the bottom of a ship. Specifically, the "corner" where the bottom meets the side.

Bloom
Thick mass of iron ready for working into bars, sheets or beams.

Boiler
Steam generator. Large iron drum to create steam to drive machinery.

Boom
Horizontal SPAR used at foot of sail or for a derrick. Also, string of logs fastened end-to-end for enclosure of a log raft.

Bow
Front of a ship.

Breeches-Buoy
A lifesaving device using a harness suspended from overhead lines to lift survivors from shipwrecks. The lines are fired out to the wreck with a Lyle Gun.

Bulk Freighter
200- to 1,000-foot ship designed to carry loose cargo such as coal, ore, limestone or grain, which is simply dumped into HOLDS.

Bulwarks
Solid rail around the DECKS of a ship. Protective extension of ship's side which runs from deck to rail.

Bulkhead
Wall or partition between portions of ship's hull.

Bunker
Space for storage of fuel, such as coal or oil.

Canaller
A ship designed to pass through the locks of the St. Lawrence River canals. From 1845 to 1884 measuring 145 x 26 feet; from 1884 to 1958 measuring 254 x 45 feet; and since 1958 measuring 730 x 75 feet.

Capsize
To roll onto one side or to turn over.

Capstan
A type of winch stood vertically. Deck device used to haul on heavy lines for mooring, towing or handling sails, using several deck hands with long wooden bars.

Chains
Anchor chains, or steering chains. Used to connect steering wheel with rudder.

Companionway
Deck opening for a stair or ladder.

Composite
Method of constructing ship's hulls, using metal frames and wooden planking.

Consort
A towbarge.

CURV III
Cable Controlled Underwater Recovery Vehicle. See ROV.

Davit
Small fixed derrick used to raise and swing out lifeboats.

Decks:
Boat – Deck where lifeboats are carried, usually upper deck. Often a short one.
Hurricane – Highest deck. Can be same as weather or boat deck.
Main – Lowest full-length deck in a ship's hull.
Spar – In BULK FREIGHTERS, the upper full-length deck. Where HATCHES are located.
Weather – Highest decks, those exposed to weather.

Derelict
A ship that has been abandoned. Out of control.

Fore-and-Aft
Running in a front-to-back direction, BOW to STERN. Schooner-rigged as opposed to square-rigged sailing vessel.

Forecastle (foc's'le)
Raised portion of a ship's BOW, used for windlass and anchor stowage in modern vessels, largely for crew quarters in 19th-century craft.

Founder
To fill and sink. To swamp.

Fresnel Lens
A large lens with a surface composed of many small lenses arranged to focus light on a single point. The orders of lenses range from First Order (largest) to Seventh Order. The Great Lakes lighthouses used Second to Fifth order lenses.

Gaff
Horizontal SPAR standing out from a mast and used to suspend top of a FORE-AND-AFT sail.

GPS (Global Positioning System)
A satellite-based navigation system for ships and aircraft, which provides accurate locational data.

Hatch
Deck opening, usually for loading cargo.

Hawser
Anchor line or towing line. Heavy rope, cable or chain.

Hold
Portion of ship's hull used for carrying and stowing cargo.

Hoodoo
A person or thing that brings bad luck; the bad luck itself.

Jettison
To throw overboard.

Jib
Headsail. Small triangular sail carried forward of ship's FOREmast.

Jibboom
Light SPAR that projects out over a sailing ship's BOW to carry the headsails (JIBS), fixed on the end of the heavier bowsprit. FOREmost feature of a sailing vessel.

Keel
The backbone of a ship. A girder which runs down the centerline in a ship's bottom, from STEM to STERN.

Lighter
A small salvage vessel used to remove cargo from a ship in distress. To remove cargo.

LORAN
"LOng RAnge Navigation;" an electronic positioning system for ships and aircraft, which provides accurate locational data.

Lumber Hooker
A ship especially designed for transporting wood and wood products.

Master
Captain.

Mate
Assistant to Captain.

Mizzen
Third mast in a three-masted sailing craft.

Oakum
Loose hemp fibers, often soaked in water repellents, used to caulk the seams of ships.

Oilskins
Cotton garments waterproofed by repeated coats of linseed oil.

Picket Boat
Class of small, gasoline-powered patrol vessels measuring about 40 feet in length.

Port
Left side of a vessel when facing ship's BOW.

Propeller
Screw used to drive a ship through the water. Type of ship driven by a screw, usually a "passenger and freight propeller."

Pyros
Slang or jargon for pyrotechnical devices like flares.

Purser
Ship's officer responsible for passenger tickets and ship's books.

Radar
Electronic device using transmitted and reflected radio waves to locate objects such as ships, obstructions or shoreline features for navigation.

Reef
Shallow area with rocky bottom.

Rigging
Wire or hemp rope used to support masts or to operate sails. Also stays for smokestack, etc.

ROV (Remotely Operated Vehicle)
An underwater device equipped with cameras and/or a manipulating arm, operated from the surface.

Schooner
Sailing craft with two or more masts, rigged with FORE-AND-AFT sails, 60 to 200 feet long.

Scow
Square-built vessel with flat sides, usually a flat bottom.

Scuttle
To sink a ship, usually by opening the sea cock, a water intake valve in the engine room.

Shoal
Shallow, sandy or muddy spot in a body of water.

Skiff
Rowboat.

Sloop
Sailing craft with one mast, ordinarily no more than 40 feet in length.

Soundings
Depth measurements.

Spar
A pole or mast used to support or spread sails or to carry lights or flags.

Starboard
Right side of a vessel when facing ship's BOW.

Steambarge
A small wooden ship used for carrying lumber products. Single-decked steamer of 130 to 200 feet with raised poop deck.

Stem
FOREmost portion of the BOW of a ship. The vertical member to which side plates are fastened at the BOW.

Stern
After (rear) end of a ship.

Steward
Officer in charge of passengers' meals and accommodations.

Strand
To run ashore or aground. To become stuck on an obstruction or a beach.

Superstructure
Cabins or "upper works" of a vessel. That part which projects above the hull.

Surfboat
Small rescue craft meant to be launched from a beach, carried on a beach-cart or trailer, usually horse-drawn. Powered by oars or small gasoline engine.

Tons:
 Displacement – Actual weight of a ship where one ton equals 2,000 pounds.
 Deadweight – Weight of cargo.
 Register – One ton equals 100 cubic feet of space (not weight).
 Gross – Entire capacity of ship.
 Net – Capacity of ship's earning spaces.

Topmast
Upper portion of a two-piece mast.

Tow
A consort or barge towed behind a steam vessel. Act of towing or pulling a second vessel.

Trough
The low point between two waves. Being "caught in the trough" means to become helplessly out of control by swinging crosswise to the waves.

Ways
Two or more inclined rampways on which a ship's hull slides during a launching.

Whaleback
Unusual ship design with steel hulls and rounded DECKS introduced by Captain Alexander McDougall of Duluth in 1888. McDougall's American Steel Barge Company built whaleback barges and steamers between 1888 and 1896. Several were also built on the East Coast.

Yawl
Small SKIFF or lifeboat. In modern parlance a two-masted sailing craft with a short MIZZEN mast astern of the rudder post.

Endnotes

CHAPTER ONE

[1]Interview, unidentified, March 10, 1999.

[2]Charles K. Hyde, *The Northern Lights* (Lansing, Michigan: TwoPeninsula Press, 1986), pp. 109-110; Seul Choix Point Lighthouse File, Stonehouse Collection; Interview, Marilyn Fischer, October 1997.

[3]Stonehouse File.

[4]*Annual Reports, U.S. Lighthouse Service*, various issues, *Daily Mining Gazette* (Houghton, Michigan), April 14, 1973.

[5]Correspondence, Ted Wagner, October 30, 1997.

[6]Interview, Lynn Carr, August 16, 1995.

[7]Interview, Robert J. Cichocki, October 8, 1999.

[8]"Haunting of Eagle Harbor Lighthouse in the Upper Peninsula of Michigan," [www.exploringthenorth.com/eagleharbor/haunted.html]; Stonehouse files; interview, August 27, 1999, unidentified.

CHAPTER TWO

[9]Interview, unidentified; Stonehouse Collection.

[10]Ronald Findlay, "The Lighthouse and Shipwrecks, Thirty-Mile Point," *Inland Seas*, (Summer 1996), p. 154; Stonehouse Collection; David D. Swayze, *Shipwreck*, (Boyne City, Michigan: Harbor House Publishers, 1992), p.177.

[11]Geri Rider, *Ghosts of Door County, Wisconsin* (Sioux City, Iowa: Quixote Press, n.d.), pp.31-34.

[12]Correspondence, unidentified to author, dated September 1, 1998.

CHAPTER THREE

[13]Interview, unidentified, March 1998; David D. Swayze, *Shipwreck* (Boyne City, Michigan: Harbor House Publishers, 1992), p. 165.

[14]Interview, July 22, 1997, unidentified.

[15]*Rochester Democrat and Chronicle* (Rochester, New York), May 13, 1921.

[16]Chuck and Sue Glisch, "Pultneyville, A Harbor of Shadows and Spirits," *Great Lakes Cruiser,* October 1995, pp. 124-25, 29-30; Arthur Pound, *Lake Ontario* (New York: Bobbs-Merrill Company, 1945), pp. 257-258, 268; Rebekah M. Porray, "Haunted House in Wayne County," (unpublished manuscript, n.d.), pp. 5-8, 27-29.

[17]Interview, unidentified, July 15, 1997.

[18]Marion Kuclo, *Michigan Haunts and Hauntings* (Lansing, Michigan: Thunder Bay Press, 1992), pp. 119-123.

[19]www.graveyards.com/calvary/

[20]*Saginaw Daily Courier* (Saginaw, Michigan), November 16, 1873.

[21]*Oswego Palladium* (Oswego, New York), April 18, 1877; Arthur Pound, *Lake Ontario* (New York: Bobbs-Merrill Co., 1945), pp. 78, 103, 245-248, 257.

[22]"Oscar of the Crosswinds," *Great Lakes Cruiser,* October 1995, pp. 34-35.

[23]Nancy Roberts, *Civil War Ghost Stories and Legends* (University of South Carolina Press, 1992), pp. 1-9; Kathleen Warnes, "Confederate Prisoners of War on Lake Erie," *Inland Seas*, (Winter 1996), pp. 302-310.

[24]Chris Woodyard, *Haunted Ohio III: Still More Ghostly Tales From the Buckeye State* (Beavercreek, Ohio: Kestrel Publications, 994), pp. 104-105.

[25]*Sturgeon Bay Expositor,* February 4, 1876; Stonehouse files.

[26]Roy L. Dodge. *Michigan Ghost Towns* (Glendon Publishing: Tawas City, Michigan, 1973), pp. 134-137.

[27]Interview, unidentified, July 20, 1999.

CHAPTER FOUR

[28]*Manistique Courier* (Michigan), December 15, 1899.

[29]C.H.J. Snider, "Schooner Days," *Toronto Evening Telegram,* June 29, 1935.

[30]Stonehouse Collection.

[31]Interview, unidentified; *Weekly Maritime News,* n.d.

[32]Stonehouse Files.

CHAPTER FIVE

[33]John M. Mills, *Canadian Coastal and Inland Steam Vessels, 1809-1930.* (Providence, Rhode Island: Steamship Historical Society of America, 1979), p. 30; *Oswego Commercial Times* (Oswego, New York), May 15, 1861.

[34]Rev. Peter J. Van der Linden, *Great Lakes Ships We Remember* (Cleveland: Freshwater Press, 1979), p. 292; Stonehouse Collection.

[35]David D. Swayze, *Shipwreck* (Boyne City, Michigan: Harbor House Publishers, 1992), p. 172; Rev. Peter Van der Linden, ed., *Great Lakes Ships We Remember III* (Cleveland, Ohio: Freshwater Press, 1994), pp. 270-271.

[36]C.H.J. Snider, "Schooner Days," *Toronto Telegram,* December 8, 1934, CLXV; Swayze, *Shipwreck,* p. 87.

[37]*Detroit Free Press,* July 3, 1909.

[38]George W. Hilton, *The Great Lakes Car Ferries* (Howell-North: Berkley, California, 1962), pp. 195-196, 118-120, 124-128; Rev. Peter Van Der Linden, *Great Lakes Ships We Remember II* (Cleveland: Freshwater Press, 1984), p.p. 311-312.

[39]Arthur C. and Lucy F. Frederickson, *Frederickson's History of the Ann Arbor Auto and Train Ferries* (Frankfort, Michigan: Gull's Nest Publishing, 1994); Hilton, *Car Ferries,* pp. 82, 89-90, 95-97; Van der Linden, *Great Lakes Ships We Remember II,* p. 28.

[40]*Daily Mining Journal* (Marquette, Michigan), December 12, 13, 1892; Mansfield, pp. 867-868; *Weekly Mining Journal* (Marquette, Michigan), December 17, 1892.

[41]Dwight Boyer, *Great Stories of the Great Lakes* (New York: Dodd, Mead and Co. 1966), pp. 75-81; *Chicago Inter-Ocean,* November 6, 1874; Cleary, *Superstitions,* p.21; Erik Heyl, *Early American Steamers, Volume IV* (Buffalo, New York: Erik Heyl, 1965), pp. 75-77; William M. Lytle and Forrest R. Holdcamper, compilers, *Merchant Steam Vessels of the United States* (Staten Island, New York: Steamship Historical Society of America, 1975), p. 255; Mansfield, *History,* p. 880.

[42]C.H.J. Snider, "Schooner Days," *Toronto Telegram,* December 1, 1934, CLXIV.

[43]C.H.J. Snider, "Schooner Days," *Toronto Telegram,* CXLIX; *Chicago Inter-Ocean,* May 18, 1890.

[44]Walton, box 4.

[45]Karl Baarslag, *Coast Guard to the Rescue* (New York: Farrar and Farrar, 1936), pp. 222-232; John O. Greenwood, *Namesakes 1930-55* (Cleveland: Freshwater Press, 1978), p. 259; John H. Wilterding, Jr. *McDougall's Dream, the American Whaleback* (Duluth, Minnesota: Lakeside Publications, 1969), pp. 41-42.

[46]Mansfield, *The History of the Great Lakes, Volume I,* (J.H. Beers: Cleveland, Ohio, 1899), pp. 659-660; Stonehouse Collection; David P. Swayze, *Shipwreck,* (Harbor House Publishing: Boyne City, Michigan, 1992), pp. 103-104.

CHAPTER SIX

[47]Correspondence, Ted G. Wagner to author, October 30, 1997.

[48]Stonehouse Collection.

[49]Interview, July 7, 1998, John Tregembo.

[50]Donald L. Cannery, *U.S. Coast Guard and Revenue Cutters, 1790-1935* (Annapolis, Maryland: U.S. Naval Institute Press, 1995), p. 60; *Grand Traverse Herald* (Traverse City, Michigan), June 12, 1899, June 25, 1917; *Record of Moments, U.S. Coast Guard, 1790-1933* (Treasury Department: Washington, DC, 1989), pp. 277-282.

[51]*Detroit Free Press*, May 5, 1902.

[52]*Mining Journal* (Marquette, Michigan), September 6, 1998.

[53]Stonehouse Files.

[54]James L. Donahue, *Steaming Through Smoke and Fire, 1871* (Sanilac, Michigan: James L. Donahue, 1990), p. 85.

[55]*Detroit Free Press*, January 2, 1999.

[56]Logbook, Light Station at North Point, Grand Island, Lake Superior, July 22, 1872, NARA, RG26.

[57]Logbook, Presque Isle Lighthouse, Lake Ontario, February 18, 1880, NARA, RG 26.

CHAPTER SEVEN

[58]Frederick Stonehouse, *Lake Superior's Shipwreck Coast* (Au Train, Michigan: Avery Studios, 1985), pp. 174-178, 181-183; David D. Swayze, *Shipwreck* (Boyne City, Michigan: Harboridge Press, 1982), p.199.

[59]William C.S. Pellowe, *Tales From a Lighthouse Cafe* (Adrian, Michigan: Raisin River Publishing, 1960), pp. 77-78.

[60]Interview author and Dennis Hale, October 1993, November 1995; Tim Juhl, Pat and Jim Stayer, *Sole Survivor, Dennis Hale's Own Story* (Lakeshore Charters and Marine Exploration: Lexington, Michigan, 1996), pp. 31-46: Stonehouse Files; U.S. Coast Guard, *Marine Board of Investigation Report, SS* Daniel J. Morrell; Rev. Peter Van der Linden, *Great Lakes Ships We Remember*, (Cleveland, Ohio: Freshwater Press, 1979), pp. 298-299.

[61]*Duluth Evening-Herald*, September 14, 1905; *Duluth News-Tribune*, September 4, 5, 6, 8, 12, 18, 26, October 20, 28, 1905.

[62]*Alone in the Night*, www.lynximages.com/robbed.htm

[63]Stone, *Lake Erie*, pp. 95-96, 137.

[64]Stanley Newton, *The Story of Sault Ste. Marie*. (Sault Ste. Marie, Michigan: Sault News Printing Co., 1923), pp. 50-51.

[65]Newton, p. 41.

[66]Barbara Chisholm and Andrea Gutsche, Superior, *Under the Shadows of the Gods*. (Toronto: Lynx Images, 1998), pp. 24-25; Stonehouse Files.

[67]*Green Bay Advocate* (Green Bay, Wisconsin), May 29, 1866.

[68]Unattributed.

[69]Unidentified Interview, July 23, 1995.

[70]*World Maritime News*, October 10, 1997.

[71]*Oswego Palladium*, November 27, 1972.

CHAPTER EIGHT

[72]*Marine Review*, Vol. IX, No. 21, May 24, 1894, p. 6.

[73]C.H.J. Snider, "Schooner Days," *Toronto Telegram*, June 27, 1934, CXXIII.

[74]*Canadian Coastal and Inland Steam Vessels 1809-1930*, p. 124; John Columbo, *Mysterious Canada* (Toronto: Doubleday, 1988), pp. 145-146; C.N.J. Snider, "Schooner Days" *Toronto Telegram*, January 31, 1953, MXC, February 7, 1953, MXCI; W.R. Williams, "The Gale-Shattered *Waubuno*," *Inland Seas* (Spring 1965), pp. 52-55.

[75]Fred Landon, *Lake Huron* (New York: Bobbs-Merrill, 1944), p. 322.

[76]Landon, *Lake Huron*, p. 311.

[77]*Buffalo Express*, May 21, 1874.

[78]*Detroit Free Press*, June 21, 1888.

[79]J.A. Bannister, "The White Sails of Dover," *Inland Seas*, Spring 1940, pp. 20-21.

[80]C.H.J. Snider, "Schooner Days," *Toronto Telegram*, June 28, 1945, DCXCVII.

[81]Dwight Boyer, *Strange Adventures of the Great Lakes*,(New York: Dodd, Mead and Co., 1974), p. 41.

[82]Boyer, *Strange Adventures*, pp. 48-49.

[83]Cleary, *Superstitions*, p. 179.

[84]*Toronto Evening Telegram*, May 16, 1931.

[85] Walton, box 4.

[86] Walton, box 4.

[87] C.H.J. Snider, "Schooner Days," *Toronto Telegram*, May 16, 1931, XVI.

[88] Walton, box 4.

[89] C.H.J. Snider, "Schooner Days," *Toronto Telegram*, June 13, 1931, XX; Larry Staples, *Wilderness and Storytelling* (Ottawa: National Museum of Canada, 1981), p. 125.

[90] Walton, box 7.

[91] James Donahue, *Steamboats in Ice 1872* (Cass City, Michigan: Anchor Publications), 1995, pp. 121-122.

[92] *Detroit Free Press*, October 30, 1857.

[93] *Detroit Free Press*, September 8-9, 1901; *Port Huron Daily Times* (Port Huron, Michigan), September 9, 1901.

[94] Bentley Historical Library, University of Michigan, Ivan Walton Collection, Box 4.

[95] Walton Collection, Box 4.

[96] *Oswego Palladium,* June 10, 1873.

[97] *Detroit Free Press,* July 1, 1887.

CHAPTER NINE

[98] *Oswego Palladium* (Oswego, New York), September 14, 1821, July 1, 1833.

[99] *Commercial Press* (Pultneyville, N.Y.) September 1867.

[100] *Detroit Free Press,* August 9, 1867.

[101] Letter September 12, 1999, unidentified; interview September 15, 1999, unidentified.

[102] *Detroit Democratic Free Press,* May 13, 1835.

Bibliography

BOOKS

Annual Reports of the U.S. Lighthouse Service, various issues, Washington, DC: Government Printing Office.

Baarslag, Karl. *Coast Guard to the Rescue*. New York: Farar and Farar, 1936.

Boyer, Dwight. *Great Stories of the Great Lakes*. New York: Dodd, Mead and Co., 1966.

— *Lakes*. New York: Dodd, Mead and Co., 1974.

Cannery, Donald L. *U.S. Coast Guard and Revenue Cutters, 1790-1935*. Annapolis, Maryland: U.S. Naval Institute Press, 1995.

Chisholm, Barbara and Gutsche, Andrea. *Superior, Under the Shadows of the Gods*. Toronto: Lynx Images, 1998.

Clary, James. *Superstitions of the Sea*. St. Clair, Michigan: Maritime History in Art, 1994.

Columbo, John. *Mysterious Canada*. Toronto: Doubleday, 1988.

Donahue, James L. *Steaming Through Smoke and Fire, 1871*. Sanilac, Michigan: James L. Donahue, 1990.

— *Steamboats in Ice 1872*. Cass City, Michigan: Anchor Publications, 1995.

Frederickson, Arthur C. and Lucy F., *Frederickson's History of the Ann Arbor Auto and Train Ferries*. Frankfort, Michigan: Gull's Nest Publishing, 1994.

Greenwood, John O. *Namesakes 1930-55*. Cleveland: Freshwater Press, 1978.

Heyl, Erik. *Early American Steamers, Volume IV*. Buffalo, New York: Erik Heyl, 1965.

Hilton, George W. *The Great Lakes Car Ferries*. Berkley, California: Howell North, 1962.

Hyde, Charles K. *The Northern Lights*. Lansing, Michigan: TwoPeninsula

Press, 1986.

Juhl, Tim; Stayer, Pat and Jim. *Sole Survivor, Dennis Hale's Own Story*. Lexington, Michigan: Lakeshore Charters, 1996.

Kuclo, Marion. *Michigan Haunts and Hauntings*. Lansing, Michigan: Thunder Bay Press, 1992.

Landon, Fred. *Lake Huron*. New York: Bobbs-Merrill, 1944.

Lyle, William M. and Holdcamper, Forrest R., compilers. *Merchant Steam Vessels of the United States*. Staten Island, New York: Steamship Historical Society of America, 1975.

Mansfield, J.B. *History of the Great Lakes*. Chicago, 1899.

Mills, John M. *Canadian Coastal and Inland Steam Vessels, 1809-1930*. Providence, Rhode Island, Steamship Historical Society of America, 1979.

Newton, Stanley. *The Story of Sault Ste. Marie*. Sault Ste. Marie, Michigan: Sault News Printing Co., 1923.

Pellowe, William C. S. *Tales From a Lighthouse Cafe*. Adrian, Michigan: Raisin River Publishing, 1960.

Pound, Arthur. *Lake Ontario*. New York: Bobbs-Merrill, 1945.

Rider, Geri. *Ghosts of Door County, Wisconsin*. Sioux City, Iowa: Quixote Press, nd.

Roberts, Nancy. *Civil War Ghost Stories and Legends*. Columbia, South Carolina: University of South Carolina Press, 1992.

Staples, David. *Wilderness and Storytelling*. Ottawa: National Museum of Canada, 1981.

Stone, Dave and Frew, David. *Waters of Repose, The Lake Erie Quadrangle*. Erie, Pennsylvania: Erie County Historical Society, 1993.

Stonehouse, Frederick. *Lake Superior's Shipwreck Coast*. Au Train, Michigan: Avery Color Studios, 1985.

Swayze, David D. *Shipwreck*. Boyne City, Michigan: Harbor House Publishers, 1992.

U.S. Coast Guard. *Record of Moments, U.S. Coast Guard, 1790-1933*. Washington, DC: Treasury Department, 1989.

Van der Linden, Fr. Peter., ed. *Great Lakes Ships We Remember*. Cleveland: Freshwater Press, 1982.

— *Great Lakes Ships We Remember II*, Cleveland: Freshwater Press, 1984.

— *Great Lakes Ships We Remember III*. Cleveland: Freshwater Press, 1994.

Wilterding, John H. *McDougall's Dream, The American Whaleback*. Duluth, Minnesota: Lakeside Publications, 1969.

Williams, J.R., "The Gale-Shattered *Waubuno*," *Inland Seas*, Spring, 1965.

Woodyard, Chris. *Haunted Ohio III: Still More Ghostly Tales From the Buckeye State*. Beavercreek, Ohio: Kestrel Publications, 1994.

COLLECTIONS

Ivan Walton Collection, Bentley Historical Library, University of Michigan.

Stonehouse Collection, various files.

GOVERNMENT DOCUMENTS

United States Coast Guard. "Marine Board of Investigation Report, SS *Daniel J. Morrell*."

INTERNET SOURCES

"Alone in the Night," www.lynximages.com/robbed.htm

Graveyards graveyards.com/calvary/

"Haunting of Eagle Harbor Lighthouse in the Upper Peninsula of Michigan," www.exploringthenorth.com/eagleharbor/haunted.html April 17, 1999.

INTERVIEWS

Lynn Carr, August 16, 1995.

Marilyn Fischer, October 1998.

Dennis Hale, October 1993; November 1995.

John Tregumbo, July 7, 1998.

Ted Wagner, October 30, 1997.

NEWSPAPERS

Buffalo Express, May 21, 1874.

Chicago Inter-Ocean, November 6, 1874.

Commercial Press, September 1867.

Detroit Democratic Free Press, May 13, 1835.

Detroit Free Press, June 21, 1888; May 5, 1902; July 3, 1909; September 8-9, 1987; January 2, 1999.

Duluth Evening-Herald, September 14, 1905.

Duluth News-Tribune, September 4-6, 8, 12, 18, 26, October 20, 28, 1905.

Grand Traverse Herald, June 12, 25, 1917.

Green Bay Advocate, May 29, 1866.

Manistique Courier, December 15, 1899.

Marquette Mining Journal, December 12-13, 1892; September 6, 1998.

Oswego Commercial Times, May 15, 1861.

Oswego Palladium, September 14, 1821; July 1, 1833; April 18, 1877.

Port Huron Daily Times, September 9, 1901.

Rochester Democrat and Chronicle, May 13, 1921.

Saginaw Daily Courier, November 16, 1873.

Sturgeon Bay Exposition, February 4, 1876.

Toronto Telegram, various dates.

Weekly Mining Journal, December 17, 1892.

World Maritime News, October 10, 1997.

PERIODICALS

Bannister, J.A., "The White Sails of Dover." *Inland Seas*. Spring 1940.

Findlay, Ronald, "The Lighthouse and Shipwrecks, Thirty-Mile Point." *Inland Seas.* Summer 1996.

Glisch, Chuck and Sue. "Pultneyville, A Harbor of Shadows and Spirits." *Great Lakes Cruiser* magazine. October 1995.

Marine Review. Volume IX, Number 21, May 24, 1894.

"Oscar of the Crosswinds." *Great Lakes Cruiser Magazine.* October 1995.

Warnes, Kathleen. "Confederate Prisoners of War on Lake Erie." *Inland Seas.* Winter 1996.

Unpublished Material

Porray, Rebekah M. "Haunted Houses in Wayne County." nd.

Index

187

About the Author

Frederick Stonehouse holds a Master of Arts degree in history from Northern Michigan University, Marquette, Michigan, and has authored 16 books on Great Lakes maritime history. Among them  are his first *Haunted Lakes, Wreck Ashore: the U.S. Life-Saving Service on the Great Lakes* and *Shipwreck of the* Mesquite: *Death of a Coast Guard Cutter,* published by Lake Superior Port Cities Inc., and *The Wreck of the* Edmund Fitzgerald.

He has also been a consultant for both the U.S. National Park Service and Parks Canada.

His articles have been published in *Lake Superior Magazine, Skin Diver* and *Great Lakes Cruiser* magazines and *Wreck and Rescue Journal.* He is a member of the Board of Directors of the Marquette Maritime Museum and the U.S. Life-Saving Service Heritage Association. He teaches Great Lakes Maritime History as adjunct faculty at Northern Michigan University and currently is instructing a web-based course on Great Lakes lighthouses. He has appeared as an on-air expert for the History Channel and *National Geographic Explorer*, as well as numerous regional media productions. He resides in Marquette, Michigan, with his wife, Lois, and son, Brandon.

Also by Lake Superior Port Cities Inc.